Wish You Were Here

Teens Write About Parents in Prison

By Youth Communication

Edited by Autumn Spanne,
with Nora McCarthy

Wish You Were Here

EXECUTIVE EDITORS
Keith Hefner and Laura Longhine

CONTRIBUTING EDITORS
Rachel Blustain, Kendra Hurley, Marie Glancy,
Tamar Rothenberg, Hope Vanderberg, and Virginia Vitzthum

LAYOUT & DESIGN
Efrain Reyes, Jr. and Jeff Faerber

PRODUCTION
Stephanie Liu

COVER ART
Stephanie Wilson

Copyright © 2010 by Youth Communication®

All rights reserved under International and Pan-American Copyright Conventions. Unless otherwise noted, no part of this book may be reproduced, stored in a retrieval system, or transmitted in any form or by any means, electronic, mechanical, photocopying, recording, or otherwise, without express written permission of the publisher, except for brief quotations or critical reviews.

For reprint information, please contact Youth Communication.

ISBN 978-1-935552-33-8

Second, Expanded Edition

Printed in the United States of America

Youth Communication®
New York, New York
www.youthcomm.org

Catalog Item #CW18-1

Table of Contents

Part I: Teens

Wish You Were Here

Antwaun Garcia 17
> Antwaun struggles with conflicted feelings about his father, who spent most of Antwaun's childhood in and out of prison.

Dealing With It

Linda Rodriguez 22
> Linda interviews several boys in a support group for youth with incarcerated parents.

Forgiving Doesn't Have to Mean Forgetting

Rita Naranjo 25
> As she gets older, Rita feels more sympathy for her drug-addicted mother, which helps her let go of some of her anger over being abandoned.

My Hero Behind Bars

Mary Fory 30
> Mary's father is in jail, awaiting sentencing. She describes her sadness and desperation.

Staying Connected

Youth Communication 36
> An expert explains how incarcerated parents and their kids can stay connected and why that's so important.

Contents

Doomed to Repeat the Past?
Antwaun Garcia 39
> Why kids who have parents in prison are at risk of ending up in prison themselves.

Seeing Through the Fog
Anonymous 40
> The writer's father is in prison, but she stays close to him through letters, phone calls, and visits.

Tears of a Clown
Eugene Han 45
> Eugene's carefree persona masks the pain of a childhood burdened by adult responsibilities, including an incarcerated mother.

Pen Pals
Stevisha Taylor 52
> Stevisha's father has been in prison since she was a young girl, but they have bonded over the years by writing to each other.

45 Minutes on the Inside
Mary Fory 56
> Mary describes the physical and emotional difficulty of visiting her father in jail.

Contents

Visiting Hours
Linda Rodriguez 59
    Linda discusses the obstacles that often prevent children from visiting their incarcerated parents.

Out of Prison and Into My Life
Dorena Belovet Ruff 62
    At age 12, Dorena begins to bond with the father she never knew.

What Makes a Father?
Youth Communication 68
    A therapist explains the role fathers play in the lives of children, and how young people can deal with absent fathers.

Part II: Parents

Back in Touch After 14 Years
Eric Benson 75
    When Eric's son Kharon is 14, he visits Eric in prison for the first time, and the two start building a relationship.

Getting Arrested Saved My Life
Sandra Jimenez 79
    When Sandra is arrested she gets sent to a drug rehab program and is able to overcome her addiction.

Contents

Dreams for My Daughter
Roger Griffin 88
> From prison, Roger tries to be a father to his young daughter during their brief visits.

Bonding from Behind Bars
Joanne Carroll 92
> Joanne, an inmate who runs workshops for her fellow parents, explains what parents need to do to avoid losing their children while in prison.

Signing Away My Son
Deborah McCabe 96
> Deborah's son is adopted while she's in prison. She is devastated when the adoptive family allows her only minimal contact with her son.

Sentenced to Be Alone
Natasha Santos 102
> Author Nell Bernstein explains how government policies make it hard for children to stay connected with incarcerated parents.

Special Delivery
Derrick Alexander 107
> Being separated from his family is especially depressing around the holidays. But Derrick keeps up his spirits by sending them special letters.

I Lost My Rights But Not My Girls
Bliss Edwards 109
> Although Bliss has given up her rights to her daughters while in prison, she has fought to maintain a connection to them.

Paying the Price
Ayinde Fair 111
> Ayinde's daughter Brittany is adopted while he is incarcerated, and he doesn't see her for five years. Recently, they've reconnected.

Sugar Daddy
Jermaine Archer 116
> Jermaine justifies dealing drugs as a way to provide for his family. But after he gets busted and ends up in prison, he feels he's failed as a father.

"I'm Sorry": A Sex Offender Tells His Story
Anonymous 120
> The author is arrested for sexually abusing his children. In jail, he gets therapy and comes to terms both with his own childhood abuse and the enormous damage he has done.

Using the Book

Teens: How to Get More Out of This Book 124

How to Use This Book in Staff Training 125

Teachers & Staff: How to Use This Book in Groups 126

Credits 128
About Youth Communication 129
About the Editors 132
More Helpful Books from Youth Communication 134

Introduction

More than 1.7 million children in the United States have a mother or father in prison. It's a separation that leaves an indelible mark on the lives of parent and child alike. Children of inmates often carry a complicated tangle of guilt, shame, fear, anger, sadness, and longing for their absent parents. This book features stories from the perspectives of both parents and teens who are coping with that absence and examining its impact on their lives.

Many of the teens' stories address the difficult struggle to reconcile an idealized version of a beloved parent with the imperfect person who cannot fully be there for them, as much as they might like to be. And the teens feel conflicted about whether to look to their parent for guidance.

In "Out of Prison and Into My Life," Dorena Belovet Ruff grows up believing that her father is dead. When she finds out that he's incarcerated, she's angry and doesn't want to let him in to her life. But after she writes him a rude letter, her father calls her and "lays down the law," telling her never to speak to him in that way again.

"That phone call was a wake-up call, like this really was my dad and, unlike my stepdad, he was in my life for good," she writes. "The fact that he was taking charge made me feel like he was a real dad, and I felt like I could start trusting him. That's when I started to forgive him."

Dorena's experience speaks to the confusion that teens—just beginning to feel a sense of independence and self-determination—feel when parents re-enter their lives and upset the delicate order they've painstakingly created out of chaos. The ease with which Dorena accepts her father's authority may feel uncomfortable to some readers, but it gives valuable insight into the powerful role, both with their absence and their presence, that parents play in these teens' lives.

How can children and incarcerated parents forge healthy

relationships under such circumstances? Even from behind bars, some parents manage to keep the lines of communication open. Several teens describe the importance of exchanging letters with their parents in prison. In "Seeing Through the Fog," one writer decides to send a letter to her father revealing that she's gay, and worries about how he'll respond. His supportive reaction shows that one of the most important things an incarcerated parent can do is show support for their children.

Through letters, artwork, and face-to-face visits, parents and children manage to cultivate fragile but determined relationships. They write about the importance of spending time together, even if it means fumbling toward a sense of family in sterile prison visiting room.

The second half of the book features stories by mothers and fathers writing from prison about their relationships with their children and the challenges of trying to reconcile their aspirations as parents with the realities of their circumstances.

Many parents share painful childhood memories of poverty, abuse, abandonment, and addiction. In prison, they are confronting these demons, tracing the effects that their difficult early lives had on the choices they made later and learning how to let go of guilt and shame in order to ultimately accept responsibility for their missteps and break the cycle.

For many of these writers, the goal of building stronger relationships with their children provides the motivation to heal and change. One young father, Roger Griffin, bonds with his toddler during visits in the prison playroom, questioning how he can give her better than he got growing up in foster care. Eric Benson seeks positive ways to reconnect with his teenage son, whom he hasn't seen in 14 years, through visits and parenting classes.

The fact is, the healing process is complex and painful. Some children never get the chance to know their parents; others witness their parents emerging from prison with lofty talk and promises, only to watch in anguish as they get sucked back into the same problems:

"Every time [it] happened I became more confused, hurt, and angry," writes Rita Naranjo. "I didn't understand why my mother kept making the same mistakes. Why was it so hard for her to stay sober and clean? Didn't my mom care? Didn't she love us and want to be with us?"

Sandra Jimenez's story provides a response to Rita's laments. After being arrested for selling drugs, Sandra is sent to a drug treatment facility. There, she manages to break the stranglehold of her longtime heroin addiction and eventually regains custody of her youngest daughter.

These stories are complicated and often uncomfortable, but also inspiring. Taken together, they are a dialogue between parents and teens struggling to figure out how to be part of each other's lives, and meet each other's needs. The aim is not to script behavior or pass judgment, but to encourage reflection and offer ways for both parents and teens to move forward.

Part I: Teens

Wish You Were Here

By Antwaun Garcia

I have seen my father go to jail so many times it's not even funny.

When I was living in the Harlem, in Manhattan, my father was doing his thang, selling on the streets. I didn't have a problem with it, because I saw it as my father did: the only way to survive.

My father wasn't born with a silver spoon in his mouth, so any way that would make him money, my father was about it. Maybe he could have gone and got a job and worked the typical 9-to-5. Some reason, that didn't work for him, and even if it did, he probably wouldn't have been able to find work because of his police record.

Once I saw my father actually get arrested. I was about 6 or 7 and we were in front of my building. My parents would fight over something stupid. Then the argument would get more tense. That scared me—when two stubborn people like my parents were in the same room fighting, it might get ugly. Somehow this argument got physical and led to the streets, both of my parents yelling at one another. One thing led to another. Someone called the cops and the next thing I knew the police were there, trying to calm my father down.

But talking and trying to reason with my father just didn't work, so the police trying to calm him down was pointless. After my moms told the police the whole story of what went down, I stood there scared, frustrated and nervous. I didn't know what to do. Who was I to go to? I didn't want to play favorites between my parents, that isn't right. So I stood alone, watching the anger between two people I loved fly back and forth.

Even though I hated him for not being in my life as much I wanted him to be, I needed him, too.

As police clipped those silver bracelets on my father, tears ran down my face. I didn't want to see my father leave, but what was I to do? I wanted to jump in and help free my father, but all I could do was stand there, not moving an inch.

They put my father head-first in the car and then he sat there in back, mad as hell. My Uncle Mike came after me to make sure I didn't do anything stupid like chase after my father. My uncle knew I would do anything for my father.

Before the police car pulled off, my father and I stared at each other with the same mad intense face. Then he winked at me, like it was a sign of something. Of what I have no idea. After he gave me that little wink, I felt strange.

A little later, I moved out with my sister to my aunt's crib. Then it became hard. It was bad enough that I couldn't see my father, because he was in prison, but also hard to be in a new area and home. You never know how much you'll miss someone till they aren't there anymore. I guess that's how I felt about my father.

I used to sit there in my new room and reminisce about what my father and I used to do. When we were in Harlem, we would sit in my older brother Chic's room, and eat some of Grandma's Spanish food while watching the basketball game. My pops and I would always compete to see who would win. Then there were those times when he would teach me how to do a fade away shot like Jordan. Those were times I can never forget. No matter what bad situations you've been in, the good ones last forever.

I kept all the cards and letters my father ever wrote me from prison. I put them all in a drawer. Whenever I missed him or thought about him, I went back to the drawer and reread the letters in remembrance and would picture him saying them to me.

On my 11th birthday I was in the car going to an amusement park with my family and my aunt gave me a card from my father. I opened it. There was a rose on the outside. Inside it said, "I'm sorry, Son, I couldn't be there for your 11th birthday. I wish I could be there to see your face behind those candles, with your face smiling as you blow out those candles."

After I finished reading the card, I pulled my head back and felt the tears fall to my ears. I groaned in silence so no one would hear me. But I think my aunt did hear me, 'cause she looked back through the rearview mirror and frowned.

Even though my father was going in and out of jail, I was never scared to tell people what he did. I wasn't ashamed to say, "Yeah, he got locked up for beating someone up, or selling, or whatever." Even though I knew my father was ashamed of his past, I wasn't. To me, his past was just a sign of pain and bad thoughts. Sometimes you need to remember those things to remind you where you came from.

Later on I felt that his being in jail and absent from my life wasn't fair. It hurt our relationship. He would write letters to me, and he would write at the bottom to respond. But I never did. I didn't know what to say to him. I didn't want to say I was fine when I wasn't.

Wish You Were Here

Soon the letters stopped, and soon the thoughts of me and him stopped, too. As I got older, it was like I didn't care for him anymore. Sometimes I felt I didn't need him. I thought, "Screw him, he isn't here for me now, so I don't need him in the future." My father wasn't there to teach me about sex. He wasn't there to teach me how to talk to females, or how to play ball. So I felt like I was my own man and I would do whatever I had to do.

Then reality struck. As much I denied being anything like my father, I saw myself becoming more like him. My mother told me that, too. I started to walk like him with that little pimp, "I'm the man" walk. The way I talked reminded people of him. I love to rock jewelry just like him. That's when I realized that even though I hated him for not being in my life as much I wanted him to be, I needed him, too.

When he finally came out of jail, he came to see my baby sister Shante and me. It had been four years since we'd communicated. I was 17 and Shante was 8.

When I first saw him get off the bus, I wanted to run and hug him like I used to as a child, but then my anger came over me and it told me to just chill and lay back and see if he actually recognized me. As he was looking for me, I called his name, and he turned around and saw me.

I wanted to run and hug him like I used to, but my anger told me to just chill and lay back.

He was happy. I could see it in his face. As he gave me a hug, my arms paused a moment before hugging back. At first I felt a little happy to see him, then it was like, "Let's just see how the day goes."

As we got to the crib and my sister saw him, she ran to him and jumped on him, like he was the monkey bars or something. I was happy for my sister, because she doesn't know too much about her father, but I still felt distant.

As the day went on, my feelings changed. I was having fun with him. We chilled in the crib and just talked and laughed as we used to. The feeling at the end of the day wasn't bad. When I had to say my good-byes, it was more like, "later," meaning, "I will see you again."

Since then I've started to realize that everyone messes up. While I can never forget the past or the crap I went through with my father locked up, I am also trying to forgive him, so that I can have him in my life without being angry.

The pain ain't healed—the pain of growing up without parents around, or the pain of always hearing something negative about them like, "Your father is going back to his old ways." Just so much pain. But it also makes me stronger. Pain and guilt seem to be my only tool these days to stay alive, to strive for greatness, to write, and to be the person I am.

Antwaun was 18 when he wrote this story.
He later graduated and went on to attend college.

Dealing With It

By Linda Rodriguez

Most young people don't get to talk about how they feel when a parent is locked up. But Children's Village, a large residential treatment center in Dobbs Ferry, New York, runs two support groups where boys can talk with each other and therapists about having a parent behind bars. One group is for boys ages 10-12 and the other is for boys age 13 or older.

In the spring I went to the Children's Village campus and talked to four boys from the younger group—Donovan, Anthony, Marcus, and Keith—about their experiences. The boys told me about feeling sad, angry, lonely, and confused. Sometimes children even feel guilty for whatever little part they think they might have played in their parent being arrested—for example, opening the door to the officer who made the arrest or not being able to stop the police from taking their parent.

Dealing With It

Donovan was just 5 years old when his father was arrested. The cops came and ransacked his house "like somebody was robbing the place. There were like 10 cops. They broke down the door," he said. "I was very confused."

Anthony's father got incarcerated twice for drug use. The second time, when Anthony was 9, he was there to see the struggle: "There were eight cops but not even all of them could get him down. They had to hit him over the head," he explained. "My mom tried to block the door so I wouldn't see." But the little he did see is still fresh in Anthony's memory, and cause enough for the inner turmoil that Anthony feels about his father.

It's very common for children whose parents are locked up to have conflicted feelings about that parent. In Anthony's case, he plainly said about his father, "I love him, and I hate him."

The anger Anthony sometimes feels because he misses his father so much is strong. Before Anthony's father was locked up, they spent a lot of time together, going fishing in Coney Island, and play wrestling. The relationship with his father was particularly important to him because his mom was always working. Now that his father's in prison, Anthony said, "I always think about the good times I had with him."

The boys talked a lot about whether they should look up to an incarcerated parent. It can be confusing.

Even when a child isn't tight with the parent who's incarcerated, it often hurts to know your mom or dad is in jail. Keith said he can't even remember his father going to prison, it was so long ago. But even though he doesn't really know his dad, he's still hurt that his dad hasn't been a part of his life. "I didn't want to have another figure in his place being Big Daddy," Keith said.

A while ago, Keith's father sent him a package in the mail. The little Keith said about receiving it made it clear how much he missed his dad. "It was a box with a little basketball and some churchy stuff, little booklets, and it had a little angel on it," Keith said. "I felt good when I got it, to know that he was still doing all right. Now every night I take it out and look at the box and read what's written on it."

During the discussion, the boys talked a lot about whether they should look up to an incarcerated parent. It can be confusing. "Our parents say, 'I want you to grow up to be just like me.' Then they do something stupid and they say, 'Don't be like me,'" said Marcus, adding in frustration, "Make up your mind already!"

Some kids start acting like gangstas because they think they should follow in their parent's footsteps. On the campus, the boys said, kids earn a positive image if they have an incarcerated parent. "Most of the kids think that if you have a family member in jail that makes you tougher," said Marcus, who was 1 when his father went to jail for robbing a store. (His father still has four more years to serve.)

But the boys I talked with said that although they loved their parents, they also wanted to make different life choices than their parents made. Marcus wants to grow up to be a famous writer. Keith enjoys playing sports and aspires to be a professional football or basketball player. Anthony uses his father's example to be a peaceful person: He said that when he's around conflict, he thinks "about all the bad things my father did and I walk away."

The boys agreed that talking about their conflicted feelings in a support group helps them to sort them out. In the long run, that might also help them live their lives differently and reach for the stars. "I've had these feelings in me since my father went to jail," Keith said. "But here I get to express myself and it sort of relieves me."

Linda was 19 when she wrote this story.
She later attended college.

Forgiving Doesn't Have to Mean Forgetting

By Rita Naranjo

Growing up, my mom went through a lot. She was abused both sexually and physically. She didn't have any support or encouragement and this made my mother feel like she was worthless. That feeling was hard for her to endure, and so she started using drugs. Drugs were introduced to her as a quick high that would make the pain go away. I don't think she could ever have imagined that drugs would affect not only her life, but the lives of her future children the way they eventually did.

My mother grew up in Miami when the drug culture was at its peak, so drugs weren't hard to access. In time the drugs consumed her, mind, body, and soul, until she lost control. Because of this she had a difficult time taking care of my brothers and me.

Then my father was killed, and my mother was devastated.

She was alone, depressed, and forced to care for four young children by herself. It was all too much for her. She became even more entrenched in drugs. They were her escape from the harsh realities of her life. But they led to my brothers and me being taken away from her and placed in the foster care system. I was 4 years old. Being in foster care changed my life, to say the least.

For nine years, I was always in and out of the system because my mother was so heavily addicted. She would follow the orders of the court to get us back, but because of her lack of support and resources, she would relapse, use drugs again, and lose us.

During this time, my mom didn't have much control over what I was doing, and I didn't care about what I was doing or about the consequences. Eventually I sort of gave up on life. I thought, "Since nobody cares about me, why should I care?" I even ended up in juvenile hall a few times.

Each time I went into the system my main thought was how I wanted to go home and stay home. I loved my mother so much. All I could think about was being with her and my brothers. I had this deep longing inside me for so long.

I didn't understand why my mother kept making the same mistakes. Didn't she care about us?

In the beginning, each time she got clean I believed that it would last and we could be a family again. I was forever hopeful. Eventually I couldn't help but doubt her, because whenever I got home it wasn't long before, yep, you guessed it, right back into the system we went!

Every time this happened I became more confused, hurt, and angry. I didn't understand why my mother kept making the same mistakes. So many questions entered my mind: Why was it so hard for her to stay sober and clean? Didn't my mom care? Didn't she love us and want to be with us?

Because there wasn't anyone explaining what was going on and why, things were left open to my interpretation. I came up with my own answers and soon discovered an easy explanation.

I figured that my mother must not care, love or want us. That was the only explanation that made her behavior and addiction make sense to me.

That answer hurt me, but it also satisfied my many questions and blotted out my hopefulness that we would be together again. In some ways, that felt better than always hoping that everything would work out fine, and then being disappointed when it didn't.

During that time, when my mom said she loved me, I couldn't say it back. I did not believe her. I'd gotten to the point where I hated her. I wondered how she could say she loved me when she really didn't.

I wasn't the only one who disliked and rejected my mom because of her addiction. Everyone who dealt with my mom in any way would start forming a strong prejudice against her. I overheard some of my foster parents calling her a junkie and low life. My social worker and other people in my agency said that they didn't really care about what my mother had to say. They didn't want to hear any of her excuses, legitimate or not. All those people just couldn't understand how she could do the things she did—get her children back only to trade them again for drugs.

The way people thought about my mom took a toll on me. Not only did it convince me that my mother really didn't love me or care that we were apart, it made me feel worthless, like I was a piece of trash. My feelings and emotions were just crumpled up, stepped on and thrown away.

But little by little, as I got older, my feelings began to change. I began to suspect that it wasn't all my mother's fault. I would watch my mother in court, able to do nothing but cry. No one wanted to hear her story, and she didn't know what to say because every time she would try to explain and plead to the court they would just close their hearts and minds.

That made me feel for my mother. It made me think that the system should be kinder to her. Though I was still angry at her,

I wanted the system to give her guidance, support and resources to help her get her life in order. I started to see that while I felt at the mercy of my mother, my mother was at the mercy of the system.

My anger towards my mother began to subside and my animosity toward the system grew. I began to feel that the system helped my mom fail.

During that time, I also started thinking about my mother's life, which had been hard, like mine. I began to realize that she still carried around pain from her childhood, which led her to use drugs to escape feeling, and which had little to do with how much she did or didn't love my brothers and me.

Foster children cannot be fully helped if their parents are denied help and support.

I also began to understand how our neighborhood contributed to her starting to use again each time she got clean. She couldn't afford to live in neighborhoods where there weren't drugs all around, so she was surrounded by temptation. My mother would always end up running into someone she knew who had drugs, and because she had an addiction, she couldn't resist.

Then my brothers and I would find ourselves in a too familiar situation. Police shining their flashlights into our eyes telling us, "Wake up! You're coming with us." Then into the back of the police car, silent tears running down our faces, thoughts racing, wondering what was going to happen next.

I recognized that while my mother's addiction hurt my brothers and me, it didn't have much to do with us, and that helped make my hate toward my mother go away. But it didn't take away the hurt, and I don't think it ever will.

I still have my own pain from the past, which can come crashing back on me without warning. When it does, I hurt. I start wondering all over why my mother did the things she did. I don't think I'll ever fully understand. But even though I don't have all my questions answered, I have still gained a better understanding about my mom and her struggles. That makes it easier for me to forgive her for not being there for us and move on with less pain.

But most people don't know my mother's story. They just see the things she does and judge her by that. I bet she was never given her chance to explain her side, to explain how many painful things happened in her past and how drugs were her way of giving up on a life that had never been good to her in the first place.

I am not asking people to accept excuses from adults whose kids are in foster care and growing up without their guidance. Sometimes those things just get passed on through the generations, and it takes some dramatic intervention to stop it.

The foster care system should not only be obliged to keep children safe and to meet their needs. They should also look out for the birth parents, whether those parents are in jail or struggling with addiction. After all, foster children cannot be fully helped if their parents are denied help and support. When you help the birth parents you are also helping us, their children, and ultimately helping to ensure that we will have a more positive future.

Judging birth parents won't help break the cycle of abuse, addiction, neglect, and pain. But I believe that understanding and support really can help.

Rita was 17 when she wrote this story.

My Hero Behind Bars

By Mary Fory

Today I go to school with a big smile like every day. I sit in the classroom and everybody is laughing around me and I ask myself, what if everybody had the same problem as me, would they keep laughing?

I don't think so, because you don't feel like laughing when your father is in jail, and today is the day when he's set to be sentenced.

Today I feel very helpless because there's nothing I can do to get my father out of jail. I imagine that today he wakes up in the morning very early, something that he always does. (When he was living at home he used to wake at 8 a.m. to go to the gym.) Then he probably takes a shower and puts on his orange uniform, and then prays for a long time.

Maybe he sits down on his bed, feeling very nervous and

anxious waiting to be called outside. He is thinking that maybe today will be the final decision and that this situation will end. I think he is thinking about us, his family. He is thinking about us like he always does, and he is hoping to be with us again.

Because we're immigrants, my father is at risk of being sent back to my native country, Colombia, in South America. If he's lucky, he could stay in this country and get paroled after a few months.

Every month during the eight months that my father has been in jail, they always give him new appointments to be sentenced, and these new appointments are always new hopes for us. But each time, they postpone. We are all hoping for the final decision so we can be released from this constant worry and not feel so desperate every single day.

When my father went to jail, everything got messed up.

Today, while my father is passing through this, I'm in school trying to concentrate on what the teacher is saying and trying to show a happy face. It's hard, and I go to the computer room to write a letter to him.

I don't know how to start. I don't know what to say to make him feel good and to make everything OK when everything is really bad. I want to scream so everybody can understand what is going on. I want to cry but the tears just don't come out.

Everything started eight months ago. I was sleeping when I heard my sister tell my brother that there was a person from the FBI knocking on the door. I got out of my bed and went upstairs.

I heard a man say that he had to check my father's room to see if he had any weapons. My brother asked him where my father was and he answered, "Your father is already in the car because we are going to take him to jail." I knew my father had had trouble with the law, but I never expected this would happen.

Wish You Were Here

The night my father was arrested, I ran outside to see him, even though I didn't have shoes on and I was wearing just my pajamas. There he was, in the police car, wearing handcuffs. My father turned to me with his strong voice (I knew that he was about to cry) and said, "Do not cry, everything is going to be OK. Just bring a glass of water because I am very thirsty." His lips were very dry.

I brought him the water and some clothes. The car left and my sister started crying and screaming. I was just holding her and trying not to cry, but it was impossible. They had just taken my father away from me.

I felt desperate, I felt sad. I knew from the bottom of my heart that he was not going to be with us any time soon. I knew that if anybody makes a mistake he has to pay later on. I went to my room and I started crying and I felt a big deep hole in my heart. Since that moment I have not eaten dinner with my father again and I have not held his hand.

Often, now, I feel very disappointed about life. I try to look for answers to my questions, but then I realize that life passing is the only thing that will answer them. I also pray. I try to keep my faith and think in a positive way, but it's hard when you are not with the person you want to be with, as I want to be with my father.

Six years ago, my father told us, he agreed to do his friend a favor by driving with him to leave some weapons in an apartment. My father had explained to us that he thought there was nothing wrong with it. My father's friend was driving and he ran a red light. When the police stopped them, they started checking the car and they found these weapons, so they took my father and his friend to jail. The judge sentenced them to six months in jail. But my father was working hard to bring us to this country (we were living in Colombia), so he ran away and did not serve the time.

Perhaps my father hasn't told me the whole story, I don't know. But even if he hasn't, that wouldn't change the way I see my father or feel about him—except that I've always looked at him as a perfect person and now I realize that he's not, and that he should have been more responsible.

I am very close to my father now, but for most of the 15 years of my life, I was separated from him. When I was 2 years old, my father came to the United States to look for a job, and I didn't see him for 10 years until I moved with my mom and siblings to be with him.

Once I came to the U.S., I grew closer to my father. It felt good when I used to wake up on Saturday mornings and he was there in the living room listening to salsa and waiting for us to share that time with him. It was a pleasure to be with him. I loved when we used to talk for a long time about what was going on in the world or when we used to play Monopoly.

In my family now, I'm "the strongest one." Sometimes, though, it's hard not to show my feelings. I'm sad, angry, and scared.

When my father was arrested, everybody in the house started telling my brother, "Now you're the man of the house, you have to study and work hard." He's only 18 and now he feels he has to be a strong person always, but sometimes he can't.

One day when we were in his room, he told me, "Sometimes this room feels very big when I'm trying to figure out how to live without my father."

In my house everybody thinks my brother doesn't care a lot about my father because he doesn't write letters to him, but it is hard for him because he's not good at expressing his feelings. My brother's counselor said that what was going on now might affect him even more than us, and that's why I always talk to him and I try to understand him, because nobody in the house really knows how he is or what he feels.

My sister is the most emotional person in our family. She writes the most letters to my father, and when he went to jail, she cried every day. She got very skinny because she didn't want to eat, she didn't want to go out, she just wanted to go and visit him. Now, she still always cries when she hears a song that my father likes about a father and his daughter.

I've always been there to support my sister. I don't let her fall down. When I have to support my sister, I want to cry, too, but I don't want anybody to come and hug me and start saying things that I already know, so I don't show the way I feel.

When my father went to jail, everything got messed up. The car broke down, we were about to buy a house but then we couldn't do it. When my father was in the house he didn't let my mother work. He always worked to give us everything we needed.

After my father went to jail, my mother started looking for a job. Now she works from 1 a.m. until 7 a.m. at a factory. Friday mornings she comes home at 8 a.m., and then at 10, she has to go to work at a hair salon so she only sleeps for two hours. Then she gets home at 6 p.m. and at 1 a.m. she has to go to work at the factory again. Saturday mornings she returns to the salon.

In the factory they don't pay my mother very well, but it's the only job that she's found for now. In the hair salon they pay OK. With the two salaries we've learned how to live during this time. We live with my uncle and he's the one who has to pay the bills for the house for now. We have to try not to waste a lot of electricity or a lot of water because it's too expensive for my uncle, and I understand that, but I feel uncomfortable living in this situation.

My mother is a great person and strong, too. But now that she's the one who's in charge of this family, sometimes the situation is too much stress for her, and she screams a lot and fights with us. In my family now, I'm "the strongest one." I always keep repeating to myself that phrase. Sometimes, though, it's hard not to show my feelings. I'm sad, I'm angry, and I'm scared.

Every day I go to the gym and it helps me get some stress out. But sometimes when I go to my house and my mother is sleeping and there is nobody available to talk to, I feel lonely. In those moments I feel angry at life and I really want my father back.

Sometimes I punch the walls. I get mad at life and I get mad at my father, because I think he should have been more responsible. But then I realize that this is how life is. And when I see my sister and know that she is going to be there for me, I feel relieved.

Now I also have pressure to be more responsible. After my father went to jail, I started looking for a job, but I haven't found one yet. The only thing I want to do is work so that my mother can quit and look for another job. I have promised myself to keep being a good student and to not make my father disappointed in me. But sometimes I feel like quitting everything and not trying that hard anymore.

Mary was 16 when she wrote this story.

Staying Connected

By Youth Communication

When Elizabeth Gaynes's daughter was 6 and her son was 2, her husband was arrested and sent to prison. A few years later, she began Family Works, a program that helps fathers in prison stay connected to their kids and become better dads.

Q: How do kids feel when their parents are in prison?

A: There's a lot of shame about parents who are arrested. Children worry that other people will think there's something wrong with them, that they're the bad seed. But these kids are not more likely to be born criminals.

My children's father was arrested when they were young. My daughter told some of her friends about it, and their mothers wouldn't let them play with her anymore. She was 7 years old. She quickly learned not to tell anyone. She said he was "down south," or in the military. A lot of kids are afraid their friends will think less of them.

Q: How do kids react to visiting their parents in jail?

A: They're relieved to see that their parents are safe. From the media, they worry that their parents will be on bread and water, or that they're mistreated. There's also a lot of sadness when they have to leave. It feels bad to be told by someone to leave your father.

They're also angry. For a year, my daughter wouldn't go visit her dad. She felt he betrayed her. Kids also get angry at the corrections department and the police and other authorities, because they believe they're responsible for putting their parent in the situation.

The parent needs to let his kids know that he alone is responsible for his mistakes and behavior.

Kids usually believe their parents are innocent or are being punished much more harshly than necessary. That's especially true now with so many people going to prison for years basically because they're drug addicts. Mostly kids' reactions are both sad and angry.

But also, there's something more complicated. While prisoners aren't treated badly in front of their kids, they're treated like children, or like they're stupid and dangerous. For example, in the visiting room, there are vending machines. But inmates are not allowed to go near them or use them. There's a line they're not allowed to cross, as if they can't be trusted with 50 cents. We like to think of our parents as strong and capable. Prisoners are treated like they're 2. They're constantly belittled. It has an effect on kids. It's difficult for kids to see that.

Visiting a parent is less difficult than being cut off, though, when all the negative feelings are still there but there's not the relief and comfort of knowing that your parent thinks of you, loves and cares for you.

Not knowing your parent who is in prison, I think the impact can be worse. I feel like whether you know your parent or not, he has a big impact on you. What info kids don't have, they make up. Either that he's a bad guy or a good guy.

Q: How does Family Works try to help kids and their fathers connect?

A: Children connect with their fathers for good or for bad. We try to help fathers not even do things unconsciously that can harm kids. Like sometimes kids will feel that their father is locked up because of something the kid did. The kid says one day, "I want a new computer," and the next day the father is arrested for stealing. The kid thinks, "I shouldn't have asked for that."

The parent needs to let his kids know that he alone is responsible for his mistakes and behavior. The child didn't cause it, and couldn't stop it. We think parents should apologize to their kids. They didn't do the crime for the purpose of hurting their kids, but they weren't thinking about their kids at that moment. They didn't think about the risk to their families if they got caught.

A lot of parents, including parents who aren't in prison, have a hard time telling their children they screwed up. They want their children to look up to them, to admire them, to respect them. They think that if you admit you're wrong, the children will respect you less. But most kids appreciate their parents admitting they were wrong.

Doomed to Repeat the Past?

By Antwaun Garcia

When parents get locked up, their kids' guardians or caseworkers often worry that the kids will follow in the parents' footsteps. There's a good reason to worry—kids who have an incarcerated parent are more likely to end up in prison themselves. Half of all teens in custody have a father, mother, or close relative who has been in jail or prison, according the Bureau of Justice statistics.

Experts say it's partly because kids are dealing with the same issues—like being around drugs, or living in poverty—that landed their parents in trouble. It can also have to do with how a child felt when the parent got locked up. "It's not because their parents are telling kids to go commit crimes," says Elizabeth Gaynes, director of Family Works in New York. "It has to do with how all children idealize their parents and want to be like them. Or it's because it makes kids angry to have a parent taken away, and that's why they get in trouble."

Children usually believe that their parents are innocent, or that they're being treated too harshly. So kids who see their parents getting arrested or being treated badly by prison guards can grow up believing that police and courts are unfair—and not worth obeying.

In 2007, about 1.7 million children had a parent or other close relative behind bars, and 5 million more had parents on probation or parole. That's a lot of kids at risk of getting locked up themselves if things don't change. Some people believe it will help families stay close—and help children to learn from their parents' mistakes—if they visit them more often.

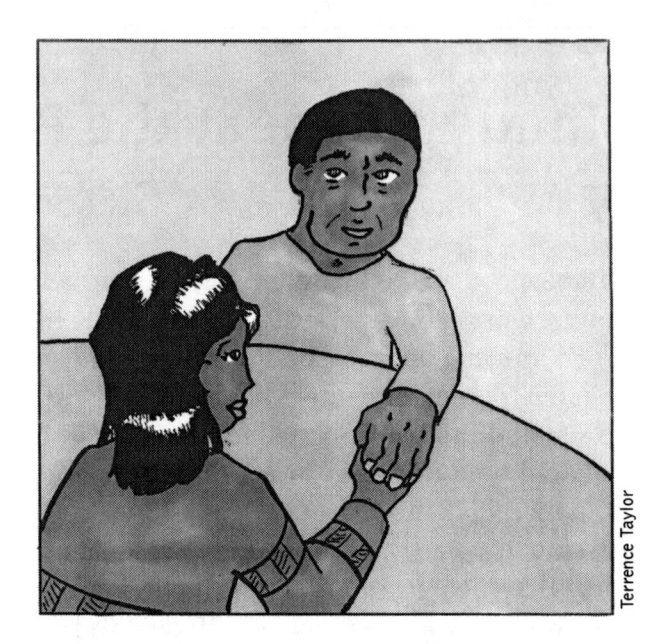

Seeing Through the Fog

By Anonymous

"Princess"—that's what my dad calls me and, growing up, it kept me smiling. My father has been incarcerated for most of my life, including the day I was born. But we have always been close.

I have a clear memory of one time when he came home right around the holidays. He got me what I wanted for Christmas: a Sony radio with four big speakers which was popular back then. On New Year's Eve we had a blast with my aunts. When the ball dropped, my dad dropped gum in my hair when he hugged me. He found it hilarious and I did, too, for a little while—until I couldn't get the gum out of my hair.

I was enjoying having him back for what I thought was going to be a long time, until the day he got arrested again. I was upset because all I could think was that it would be another couple of years before I'd see him. That put me in lost mode. I hated him for leaving, but I loved him for letting me know everything was going to be OK and he was going to be home again real soon.

All the time I was growing up, he kept in touch by mail and sometimes through phone calls. He would write me every week to let me know how things were going and ask me how everything was on my end. He always said, "How's my baby girl?" and ended with, "Princess, I love you," which often left me in tears. He sent me cards on Valentine's Day, my birthday, and Easter, and every time he did there was a letter inside.

Sometimes I would respond. Sometimes I wouldn't, not because I didn't want to, but because I had so much to tell him I felt the best way to speak to him was face to face.

The older I got, the more I missed him. Even though he was away, I still felt closer to him than to anyone else. We had so many of the same interests: we both loved writing poetry and free writing whatever came into our heads in one long stream. We're both very open with people. We even look alike. One of the times he came home, I realized we had the same nose, eyes, dimples, and lips. It was crazy—I looked like a female version of my dad. On the down side, we both have bad attitudes that are hard to control.

I also wanted him around because I was growing up with five younger half brothers who always ran to their mothers. I just wanted my father. I wanted

> **He always ended with, Princess, I love you," which often left me in tears.**

him to be there for every little problem I had. Because he was away for so long, I felt the world was against me. He always told me that when he came home, things were going to be different.

I was looking forward to that when I found out my dad was getting married to an old girlfriend of his. I was stunned. I didn't know her too well, but I felt sure that with her around, everything would change between him and me. I felt she would take him away.

By that time I was getting older and starting to go through

my own changes. I was about 14 when I started to notice I was attracted to girls more than boys. I wanted to tell my dad, but I was kind of scared. Even though he'd never been upset or disappointed with me before, there's a first time for everything. When I came out to other people, I had a "there's nothing to hide" attitude, but it was hard. In my family, people made the issue bigger than I ever thought it was.

Then I wrote to my father about it. He didn't say too much about the situation when he wrote back, but he did tell me that if that was what I wanted, he was there for me. Everybody else made it seem like it was the end of the world, but he didn't. This made me want to go see him, because I felt he would give me even more support in person.

> **I had this jealous fear that my dad was going to come home soon and my baby sister would have the childhood I'd always wanted.**

But the first time I went to see him in prison after that letter, I was kind of nervous. Besides my coming out, I thought he was going to tell me about his soon-to-be wife, who I really didn't want to know about. We started discussing all the big changes for us in the past year or so, and I was praying the things I'd heard about him getting married were just talk.

Then he pulled me aside and asked me about what I'd told him in the letter. I explained everything and he asked questions. He told me that I shouldn't ever worry about people saying things about me, because I am me and I shouldn't change myself to make anybody happy. He told me that he's not going to say I'm doing wrong, because whatever makes me happy makes him happy.

At that moment my reaction was a big, relieved sigh—I was thinking, "Wow, nice way to handle that, Daddy." I let myself go a little and took a couple of breaths, like, "I got this." He asked about a male friend that I had, Damien (not his real name). I said, "We were always just friends, not together." He knew from there that I was serious about the whole girl thing.

See, I got so much stuff from other people—stuff like, "You too pretty for that," or "You're too young." I even got, "You know you want a baby. How you going to have a baby with a girl?" Stupid things like that didn't affect me at all, but it got to me when they would say, "You going to hell, God ain't made you like that." As I see it, if God created me, he knew what was going to be in store for me. So if I'm going to hell, I'm going to have millions behind me.

When my dad said he would never tell me I'm wrong in loving who I want, it made me feel good. With all that he said to me, I had to think again about him and his girlfriend. I couldn't tell him I didn't want him to love her. I had to stand by him as much as he stood by me.

That's why I started to give her respect when I saw her, listening to her when she was speaking. To this day I do feel she does things just to have him to herself, and that I will not tolerate. But for my father's sake, I am coping.

Still, when I later found out my dad was having a baby with his future wife, I felt as if I was going to be replaced and I hated the thought of that. I worried even more when I found out the baby was going to be a girl, and I wouldn't be his only daughter anymore. I hated talking about it, or even seeing his future wife's belly. It was all coming too fast. I knew I'd have my dad on my side regardless, but so would the baby. In letters I asked my dad over and over again: "Does this mean I'm not going to be your princess no more, because I'm getting older?"

That was a joke to him. He told me I was his first daughter and always would be his princess, his baby girl, and his heart. Hearing that was the only thing that kept me smiling through the other chaos that was going on in my life. My father never looked at me differently no matter what I told him about the relationships I had with girls. Everything he told me made all the negative things other people said look like clear fog: I didn't see it, and I sure enough made it my business not to acknowledge it.

When my sister was born, I was so jealous, but I knew I had to get over it. So I asked to go to my grandma's house so I could spend a little time with her. When I finally held her, she didn't cry and I fell in love with her. I still had this jealous fear that crept up on me, that my dad was going to come home soon and she would have the childhood I'd always wanted. But I realized I was being selfish, that she didn't ask to be born and it wasn't her fault.

Today, my dad is like my best friend, even though he's still in prison.

My dad kept sending his letters, each with a thousand questions. I was happy because he continued to keep track of whoever my girlfriend was at the time, so I knew he did care and he wasn't just pushing that to the side. His openness also made me open up to him more. I started telling him things that no one else knew.

Today, my dad is like my best friend, even though he's still in prison. Don't get me wrong—my mother has always been there for me; she has kept a roof over my head and protected me, and I appreciate every bit of what she does. But my dad has made me feel more accepting of myself and that's why he gets an A+ from me.

I see no change in our relationship since he got married and had his new baby. He promised me that he wouldn't put my sister before me nor me in front of her, and he doesn't. He has been a dad to both of us and to my two brothers from his side.

And he will be home soon. I'm waiting for that. I hope he'll be staying home this time, and that we'll become even closer than we already are.

The writer was 19 when she wrote this story.

Tears of a Clown

By Eugene Han

Most people who know me would be surprised to hear that I've struggled with loneliness and depression for much of my life.

I'm always the guy who cracks a joke or adds sarcastic side comments to lighten up any conversation. I never have anything sad to say and I always try to bring people into the conversation so they won't feel left out.

But there is a deeper, more meaningful me. I've dealt with a lot of serious issues in my life—the absence of a family member, failure in school, financial instability and coming to terms with my sexuality. I may be silly and social in public, but I act this way because I don't like it when people pity me. It makes me feel sorry for myself, so I just cover all my problems.

Maybe it started when my mother was arrested on a drug charge and sent to prison when I was only 7.

I believe my mother was unjustly sentenced. While she did have a connection to a big dealer, she personally didn't deal drugs. Why didn't the courts ever consider that she was a single parent with two young children? I felt anger, sadness and frustration. It was as if they were ripping away the only support I had without a second thought. (My father had left us when I was a year old. He's never helped my family, ever.)

Before she went to jail, my mother asked my great-grandmother to move in and look after us. She did cook for us, but other than that she just sat around and watched TV. She was very old, illiterate, and crippled (she had broken her hip and had trouble walking). I always wished she wasn't handicapped, that she could have done more with us, taken us places. It was up to me to take on responsibilities normally taken care of by an adult. It became my job to pay bills, read, and translate important letters, etc.—even though I was still a little kid.

I would cry every night, wishing and hoping that my mom would return the next day.

To make matters worse, when I was in school, kids would call me f-got at times. (I guess they thought I was feminine or something.) I would cry every night, staring up at the stars from my bedroom window, just wishing and hoping that my mom would return the next day. As the years passed, her return felt more and more like an impossibility. It seemed useless to keep hoping. I felt my heart ache and sink deep within me.

I tried burying myself in my schoolwork and reading lots of books, especially mysteries, so that I wouldn't have to think too much about it all. At home, I only had my brother, and we've never been tight. We're total opposites. He did nothing to help the family out, which made me feel even more alone in my efforts. At school, I mainly kept to myself. I was never popular and I never hung out with anyone in particular. I was more of a homebody, and my responsibilities kept me busy.

When I was 14, I started feeling down and lost interest in

things—especially school. I felt too tired to get out of bed and more than ever before I felt overwhelmingly lonely. That year, our family started running out of money. No one worked in the household so we only had welfare and what was left of my mother's savings. We were scrimping, but it just wasn't enough to pay the monthly mortgage bills. So my mother, who called us from prison, decided we needed to sell our house. I was stunned. I didn't know where we would go.

To save the money we had left, my mother arranged to send us to a children's home in Kentucky. A fellow inmate had recommended it to her. My brother and I would stay in the dorms with the other kids until our house in Queens, New York was sold. Then my great-grandmother would come and the three of us would live in the guest house behind the main building.

When I heard about this, I was relieved that there would be a decent place for us to live. I hoped we wouldn't have to worry about money anymore and that I wouldn't have so many responsibilities.

My brother and I spent six months in Kentucky while my great-grandmother was still in New York. Most of the kids at the home were nice, and I felt positive that things would get better. Then my great-grandmother called to tell me that she didn't want to live with us anymore and instead wanted to return to Taiwan. When I heard this, my heart sank. Once more, I felt abandoned.

I returned to New York to find that my great-grandmother had sold the house to my aunt. My great-grandmother decided to stay a while longer, and we ended up renting the basement from my aunt.

I wasn't crazy about living with my great-grandmother again. I felt as if she'd betrayed me, promising that she would come to Kentucky and then deciding not to. But I was glad that she was staying because I had lived with her for years and at least she was familiar.

The arrangements in the basement were a little different,

though. I didn't have a bedroom. I slept on two thick blankets on top of a countertop in the bathroom. It wasn't as bad as it sounds. The bathroom was pretty big and I enjoyed sleeping in it because I had my own corner and my own little window. It made me feel better to be able to look out a window at night looking up at the stars until I fell asleep, wishing my mother was there with me.

I got back to New York in time to start 8th grade. But once again, I started feeling too tired to get out of bed for school. I was tired of how my life was, tired of how futile my fight to cope felt. I did well in school, but all I felt was, "So what?" Getting good grades didn't change my loneliness or my worrying about my family. I was so distressed that I started just staying in my "bed" all day, looking out the window, feeling hopeless about my horrid life.

Then we got kicked out of the basement. One of the neighbors had reported us to the fire department, which considers living in a basement a fire hazard. Now we had to find a new place to live. We got the most decent cheap apartment we could find. My grandmother, who came from Taiwan to help us move, persuaded my great-grandmother (her mother) to continue living with me in the new apartment. Though she was starting to annoy me, there wasn't anyone else able or willing to take her place. None of my aunts and uncles offered to help, which made me feel unwanted and unworthy of being cared for.

Though I tried hard, I barely made it through junior high. But I got into a pretty good high school, and figured I could start anew. I was much more social than before. I seemed to be a cute, funny, sweet boy without a care in the world. Everyone seemed to like me, but I felt that it was just a fake me that didn't represent my true feelings. I acted silly and carefree in public, hoping that it would rub off on my true self. The truth was I was still hurting inside, where all the drama was going on.

I had also just realized that I was gay. (Looking back on my childhood, I don't know why I hadn't figured it out earlier; I was always the little diva.) Almost as soon as I recognized my sexuality, I started "coming out" to anyone who asked. I would purposely give little hints like saying that a guy was cute. That would make people ask if I was gay and I would tell them. Most people reacted well; I guess it was never a big surprise to them.

I realized that keeping things in kept me depressed. I was embarrassed about things like my mother's incarceration, so I always made up stories if people asked where she was. But every time I told a lie, I got sad; hiding things about myself kept me down. So I decided I had nothing to hide and to be proud of myself.

My new open attitude didn't help as much as I had hoped. I still didn't find the friends I needed, because even though people said they didn't care that I was gay, I felt like no one was totally comfortable with my sexuality. I started feeling lonely again.

I got careless about my schoolwork, almost as if I had to prove to myself that I wasn't good enough. I felt really tired when the time came every day to get up and go to school, so I just didn't go. I would make up excuses to myself, like "Oh, you woke up late, so don't go to school and just say the next day that you were sick," or "I think I'm getting sick," when I had a runny nose. My grades went dooowwwnnnn.

I felt like a failure with my family, too. When I came back from Kentucky, I had tried to remake them to match an ideal image. It was an uphill battle.

My family is not known for its togetherness. My mom, uncles and aunts despise each other, never helping one another out when times get tough. They also have nasty habits. They throw trash on the ground and the men chain smoke. It also annoyed me that they didn't even try to learn English when they were in an English-speaking country.

I tried creating togetherness by calling my relatives more often. I tried to get my family to eat healthier and act more "sophisticated." I would buy all the groceries and clean the house from top to bottom. I hoped these improvements would counter our poverty. I even watched *My Fair Lady* (a movie about a poor flower girl who is taught to be "proper" by talking, walking and acting high class) to figure out how to get my family to change. But it was totally hopeless.

I had tried to improve my family, but I should've known they were beyond my control. You can't change other people; people change only when they want to. It dawned on me that maybe I was ready to change myself. I knew that I was having trouble again and I decided that I should see a counselor. I was skeptical—if I couldn't find out what was wrong by myself, how could this person do it?—but I went to my school's counselor.

I told the counselor some of the reasons I was depressed: loneliness, my family problems, and my sexuality. He suggested that I try joining a peer group for gay teens. When I showed up at the community center for a group meeting I was somewhat nervous, looking around for people who I might be able to talk to afterwards. I wanted to be accepted by the masses and along the way find myself a soul mate. I was grasping the reality of my sexuality and was excited to see how life was for other gay people.

> **I had tried to improve my family. It dawned on me that maybe I was ready to change myself.**

At the center, I met lots of people who I like and now hang with, including my best friend, Effy. Sometimes I feel as though my friends are more family than my real family. They made me feel more comfortable and gave me the courage to be loud. Before when I acted carefree and silly, I was overcompensating, trying to cover up how shy I felt. But now when I'm more outgoing and silly, it feels like the real me.

The feeling of some reassurance gave me hope. I was able to look into myself, and think more clearly about my feelings and what I wanted. I knew I wanted to be "someone" and go to college.

I still had some problems. Because I had missed so much

school, I had gotten left back. But I wanted to move forward with my life, not backward. So I dropped out of high school and took the GED and SATs.

I didn't do very well on the SATs. I hadn't studied because I was underestimating my abilities and didn't bother to try. But I didn't want to get down on myself again. I told myself, "You didn't do that great, but it's OK; now you just have to do really great in college for a chance at your dreams." I applied to colleges I thought I could get into, and with a little struggle I got accepted to Brooklyn College.

With the help and encouragement of my friends, I am slowly and successfully getting over my depression. I'm concentrating on what I need to do, like school, and I'm learning to ignore the little things that irritate me. I'm also writing in my journal every day, so there is always a way to let out my feelings. Though I no longer feel the need for the peer group, I still drop by the center once in awhile to say "hi."

My grandmother moved in with me last year, so that my great-grandmother could move back to Taiwan, which was fine with me. My mother is set to get out of prison next year, but I don't plan on living with her. I don't feel that connected to her at this point. I missed her a lot when I was younger, but now I feel like I've grown up and it just doesn't matter as much.

I've realized that I have always compared myself to others, and set ridiculous goals. And it would make me depressed if I couldn't reach my goal within a certain time. But now I know better. "Baby steps, baby steps" is what I tell myself now. I've learned that the best way to deal with my problems is to take small, positive steps towards my goals.

Eugene graduated from high school and enrolled in college in New York City.

Pen Pals

By Stevisha Taylor

One day when I was 3, my father went over to my grandfather's house. My father and grandfather had always had a bad relationship, because my grandfather beat on his wife and kids. That day, they ended up arguing over money and other business. My relatives say my grandfather had been drinking and pulled a gun on my dad. Then my dad pulled a gun on him, too. Shots were fired, my grandfather ended up dead, and my father got thrown in jail.

I was heartbroken. I lived with my father (my mom had dropped off because of drug use) and now I was being cheated of him. My father got sent to a prison far away. It meant that my father and I could never see each other.

After my father was arrested, my aunt and grandparents thought not seeing him until I was 18 was best for me, and the courts agreed. Since then, I've had to wake up each day with the hurt of knowing I will not see my father. But the amazing thing is that my dad has always been in my life.

For as long as I can remember, he has written to me. I was about 5 when I started sending him pictures I drew. I was 8 when I started writing. Most of the time we wrote about us not being able to see each other. I sent him a letter just about every other week. He'd send me birthday cards and letters and he'd tell me that he cared about me, that he loved me and would never on purpose do anything to hurt me.

Over the years, I stopped drawing but I wrote to him more and more. Now I write to him every other day and he writes to me once a week. We talk on the phone about every other week. He tells me that jail is a hard-knock life. He writes to me about his life before jail, too. He tells me that growing up was not easy. His father would beat on him and his brother. Sometimes they would try to stop their dad from beating up their mom.

When my father was a teenager, he got tired of the abuse, and one day he ran away. My father told me how hard it was leaving behind his mother and brothers. But his oldest brother helped him get away, and my dad went to live with his aunt (may she rest in peace).

When my father was growing up, he had lots of hard times to deal with, with his family and with

My father writes to me about his life, and I tell him all my secrets.

growing up black when life for blacks in this country was even rougher. Then, when he messed up, he got thrown in the clink.

My father writes to me about his life, and I tell him all my secrets. When I was younger and would tell him about my mom using drugs, he'd be upset and say that he was sorry that he wasn't there for me. When I told him I was being hurt at home, he was furious about the situation. He was mad at the world. But there was nothing he could do but tell me to be strong and hold on.

When I went into foster care, I let him know. I felt like now I was like him, just another inmate in the system, waiting to be free. Again, he apologized for not being there for me. He always blames himself for everything that's going on with me.

I feel like these years of writing and talking have bonded my father and me. All our letters make me feel like we are one. Sometimes I cry when we talk because I miss him. Other times I tell him about my life and he just listens.

Learning about my father's experiences has left me angry, but it's also made me want to make my life better, to finish school and go to college and succeed, for myself, my father, and my child. It isn't always easy.

Although the courts originally ruled that I shouldn't see my father until I turn 18, the judge allowed me a visit. I won't ever forget that day. On one of my court dates, he came to see me. The guards just sat in the room with us while we talked to each other. We caught up on a lot of things that had been going on in my life. It felt like my fairy tale wish had finally come true.

Learning about my father's experiences has left me angry, but it's also made me want to make my life better.

My dad's release date is in a couple of years. I will be so happy when he's out and we will be able to form a life together. Of course I have worries about things not working for my dad, like him not being able to find a good job, or even a part-time job, since it's hard for ex-cons to find work—especially people like my dad who have been locked up for so long.

But at least I'll be able to take care of him and we will be able to talk to each other a lot more. We'll spend father-daughter time together, and if I have a problem, I'll be able to call him late at night. I look forward to him being a part of his grandchild's life. Whatever happens, I will just be happy that he's out and that we have the chance again, after so much time apart, to be together as a family.

Stevisha was 18 when she wrote this story.

45 Minutes On the Inside

By Mary Fory

Visiting my father in prison is one of the most important moments for me. When I go to visit him I feel happy and excited. It is a wonderful feeling that I can't even explain.

In the beginning we used to go three days a week, in the afternoons when we came from school. But a few months ago our car broke down. Now we only visit him when my mother's best friend lets my mother borrow her car.

When we go, we have to make a line outside the jail and wait until other people come out. Sometimes it was terrible in the winter when the weather was really bad, but everything was worth it when we saw our father.

Once we get inside, we have to make another line and wait to be called. Then my mother, who is the only person we can go in with, has to give proof that she's our mother and give our birth certificates, too.

Women can't wear bras, and we can't wear anything that has metal, like chains, earrings, bracelets, overalls, or rings. We can't chew gum and we can't take money inside. The first time we went, I was amazed at all the things that we had to do just to see my father for 45 minutes.

After we are checked, we go to a big room where there are three big tables. Each table has 10 spaces with a number. They give us a number and we sit down to wait for my father. The inmates (which is what they call the people who are in jail) have to make a line and then they go to see their families, who are waiting for them anxiously.

My father comes and he sits behind the table. This is the best moment because I can hug him and kiss him, but it is sad sometimes because the rules say that you just can kiss him and hug him one time. If you don't follow the rules, they don't let you continue with the visit.

It's a great moment when I can see him and tell him everything about home and how much I love and miss him. He always says, "Oh, all of you look very pretty today," and he asks if there are any problems at home.

The worst moment comes when I have to say good-bye to that person who I want to be with always.

He wants to know how we are behaving, if we are doing well in school, if we are helping our mother. He always asks these kinds of questions and tells us stories about the place, and that's the way we spend our 45 minutes.

The worst moment comes when I have to say good-bye to that person who I want to be with always. It's funny when you see all the wives kissing their husbands in a desperate way, but it is also sad.

Before my father goes back to his room, he has to strip naked and get checked by the guard. I don't like knowing that he has to bend over and get checked everywhere. Still, we all have to fol-

Wish You Were Here

low the rules if we want to spend that short time with him.

I feel very restricted when I have to see him just for 45 minutes, when I used to see him every day. It's very hard when I just want to take him home with me and when I feel helpless because there is nothing I can do to take him out of there.

When I go to visit him he always shows a happy face. He has faith and he says he knows we're OK. But I know my father and I know he's not happy in that place. He says that sometimes he feels lonely and that he always thinks about us the whole day. He says that every day there is the same.

Mary was 16 when she wrote this story.

Visiting Hours

By Linda Rodriguez

One of the toughest parts of having a parent locked up is that many kids only get occasional visits—if you get any visits at all. In New York, for instance, regulations say that kids are supposed to have regular visits with an incarcerated parent, unless the judge rules that a visit would be harmful. But according to the Department of Justice, about half of incarcerated mothers and fathers say they've received no visits from their children since they've been in prison. (Close to half of incarcerated parents do have weekly contact with their kids, either by phone, mail, or through visits.)

Sometimes kids themselves don't want to go because it can be a big hassle to visit someone in prison. The visiting rooms are often noisy, crowded, and uncomfortable. Plus, there are all the security procedures. Anything or anyone brought inside the prison has to be thoroughly searched.

And kids often can't visit because a parent is locked up far away. Sixty percent of incarcerated parents are locked up more than 100 miles from home. Our government doesn't make it easy for families to stay connected.

Children may also find that visiting an incarcerated parent can feel like waving cheese in front of a mouse, and then taking it away. It can hurt even more to know that at the end of a visit, you're going home and your parent can't come with you.

Many times, though, children don't see their parent because the child's caretakers—relatives, friends or foster parents—don't want to bother, or because they think the less children know about the situation their parent is in, the better. The caretakers might also resent the incarcerated parent, and say that if parents had cared enough about their children, they'd have avoided prison. Most of the time, the foster parent or caseworker doesn't even know the parent so it makes it easier for them to say that the parent is a bad person.

> **Many times, children don't see their parent because the child's caretakers don't want to bother.**

Even if caretakers are trying to act in the child's best interest, having someone else decide that you can't see your parent can really hurt, especially if you had a close relationship with your parent. It can also mean you're left with a lot of unanswered questions.

Tanya Krupat, who runs the Children of Incarcerated Parents Program in New York, said she often sees foster parents and caseworkers trying to protect kids, but instead they wind up keeping them in the dark.

Ms. Krupat believes that children should be involved in the decision to visit their incarcerated parent. In the last few years, the Children of Incarcerated Parents Program has begun to educate caretakers about this topic. They started training caseworkers, and have also trained some foster parents. They hope to do more.

The training sessions try to help caseworkers and foster parents put aside their own feelings about people who are in jail, and focus instead on what the child wants, explains Ms. Krupat.

"The biggest barrier is the attitude toward people in prisons and jails and the type of people who wind up there," she said, adding that parents who wind up in jail are not always horrible people who committed bloody and evil crimes. "Most cases are non-violent, drug-related crimes," she said.

The program has also been working with Rikers Island (a jail in New York City) to make sure kids in foster care are able to visit their mothers and to create more child-friendly visitation days. They even have holiday parties, with food and singing and kids running around the visiting room.

Having someone else decide that you can't see your parent can really hurt.

There's no guarantee that these visits will always be positive. But more visitation time for kids does give their relationships with their parents space to grow. It gives parents a chance to explain themselves and be close to their kids, and it gives children a chance to explore their feelings and be close to their parents.

Linda was 19 when she wrote this story.

Out of Prison and Into My Life

By Dorena Belovet Ruff

One night when I was 12, my mom and I caught a bus upstate to Franklin, New York. We'd gone shopping for the trip and I'd gotten a new green corduroy jumper and matching shirt. When the bus made a pit stop, we washed up and I put on my new outfit. I was very curious and a bit nervous to see what would happen. But at least I looked fly (I thought) for my first visit to prison.

When we finally arrived, I had to take off all my jewelry, my belt, and my shoes and socks. I felt violated, not to mention disappointed about messing up my new outfit. We made it inside the visiting area, sat at our designated table and waited for his arrival.

When he came in, my mother pointed him out. My eyes wandered from left to right, trying to figure out who she was pointing at. Then I saw him, a reflection of me. My dad.

I hated him immediately. I'd gone through all of that stuff just to meet this stranger who'd never been there for me. He kept staring at me like he was reading me or trying to figure out who I was. That just pissed me off more. "Why do you keep looking at me, ugly?" I said.

He laughed.

"Yeah. Ha ha," I thought. He asked me how I was doing, how the ride was and how school was. I gave one-word answers—I couldn't stand the small talk. I needed answers to my questions, like "Why is he here?" and "Why am I here?" But I didn't ask him because I felt I should have already known the answers somehow.

Then my stepfather called the jail. He was jealous and he didn't want my mom and me visiting my father, so he told the jail that we were transferring drugs to my father. They pulled us out and strip-searched all three of us again.

When we returned to the visiting room, stripped of our dignity, I wasn't only mad at my mother's husband. I was mad at my father, too. If it weren't for him, we wouldn't have been there in the first place. When my mom and I left the prison, I was angry, disappointed, and determined not to have my father in my life.

Who was he to make plans not only for my life, but for my mother's life, and even my brothers' lives?

Before that day I'd never even known about my father. My mom had always told me that he was dead, and we never talked about him. I never even saw a photograph of him. Of course I'd wondered who my dad was, but never enough to bring it up.

For reasons I still don't know, my brother and I lived with my grandmother until she died when I was 7. Then we moved in with my mom and stepdad. I guess you could say I had a father figure, but I didn't like my stepdad or consider him a father.

Then one day when I was 12, my mom told me we were going to visit my grandmother, who she'd recently run into. I was confused—my grandmother was dead. Mom explained that she was talking about my other grandmother, on my father's side. "Wow, where did this come from?" I wondered. The idea of having another grandmother had never crossed my mind.

At her house, my grandmother sat us at the kitchen table and asked me, "Have you visited your father yet?"

"No," I said. I didn't understand what she meant. My father was dead, right? I didn't even hear what my mom and grandma talked about after that, because I kind of went into a trance, trying to make sense of what was happening. Was my grandmother talking about visiting his grave? But part of me knew she was telling me that he was alive, and that confused me.

I guess my mom took my grandmother's hint that it was time for me to meet my dad, because soon after that, she told me we were going to go see him—in jail.

My mom told me he was in jail for something he'd done when he was younger and running in the streets. He'd been there since my mom was pregnant with me. All I could think was, "A damn jail cell? This is some bull crap." No wonder my mom had told me he was dead. I just knew he must be a bad man if he was in jail, and I immediately classified him as an a--hole.

After I met him in jail, I didn't bother to continue our relationship. I figured I'd met him, I knew who he was, and that was all I needed to know. But soon after that visit, my mom and stepdad split up because of personal problems, and my mom started talking to my father on the phone.

A few months later, I was cleaning the house and I found a letter with my dad's name on it, addressed to my mom. In the letter, he said that he was going to adopt my brothers (my ex-step-father was their biological dad) and that he loved my mom and they were going to be together. When I finished reading it, I was pissed off and on a mission.

I couldn't believe the audacity of my dad to say he was going to adopt my brothers when he couldn't even get along with me. What he'd written about being with my mom was the icing on the cake. My mom had just gotten out of the relationship with my stepfather and she was vulnerable. I didn't want to see her hurt. Who was he to make plans not only for my life, but for my mother's life, and even my brothers' lives?

I responded to his letter, ignoring the fact that it wasn't even addressed to me. I told him I hated him and I thought that he was stupid, and that there was no way that he was going to adopt my brothers, so he could go to hell. He didn't write back. Instead, he called my mom and asked her to put me on the phone. Then he told me, "Don't you ever write some sh-t like that to me again."

I was shocked that a man had talked to me in that manner. My mom's husband had tried to discipline me, but I never took him seriously. I wasn't used to a man laying down the law. That phone call was a wake-up call, like this really was my dad and, unlike my stepdad, he was in my life for good. It might sound strange, but the fact that he was taking charge made me feel like he was a real dad, and I felt like I could start trusting him. That's when I started to forgive him.

He wrote to me soon after, and we started writing each other letters weekly. We found out we had a lot in common. We both liked to read and write. We were both free souls, not followers, and we both hated authority. It kind of star struck me because my mom and I don't have a lot of things in common and our personalities clash a lot. I was happy to find out that I had a parent who was like me. The more we talked, the closer we got, and the more I let go of my resentment and animosity toward him.

> **As I got close to my dad, I began to realize that I'd missed out by growing up without a father.**

When I was about 15, he made an audiotape for me. He's kind of a preacher, teacher, advisor and philosopher all in one, and he makes tapes for family members and anyone he trusts enough to become a part of the family. On the tape he gave me, he preached self-awareness and building up one's self and family. He also told me that he loved me, which made me feel happy and glad to have him as a daddy.

When he got out of jail a year later, I couldn't believe it. He'd been in jail for 16 years and there'd been rumors about him being released, but nothing official. I was elated. He and my mom never did get back together. But he and I have been road dogs since the day he got out, hanging out all the time.

When I was growing up, my stepfather wasn't worth a dime, and I figured all fathers were the same. But as I got close to my dad, I began to realize that I'd missed out by growing up without a father.

My dad feeds my mind with new ideas and introduces me to new things. He's been a vegetarian for years and one day he took me to a vegetarian restaurant, where they had all types of fake meat, like chicken, shrimp and beef, made out of soy. I'd never tasted food like that before, and it was pretty good.

He has also done so much for my self-esteem and pride. Nothing compares to him teaching me how to drive. One ordinary day last December, he came to pick me up and we were sitting in the car. I said, "I wanna drive." We'd been talking about it for a while already, so he said OK. We switched seats and the rest is history.

He's been patient and taught me everything about driving, step by step. Having him teach me to drive is special to me, because even though he missed the first 12 years of my life, now he's witnessing me grow up.

We have some of our best conversations sitting in the car. One day we were talking about a 16-year-old girl he knew who was pregnant. I guess since he got my mom pregnant early, he didn't want to see me end up the same. "You know, I have plans for you and getting pregnant isn't a part of the plan," he said.

"Yeah, I know. You don't have to worry," I said.

"Nah, I'm serious. You're graduating and going off to college and I'm proud of you for that. You don't know how happy I am to be here experiencing this with you. But it don't stop there. Your sister [his other daughter] should be in school now but because she got pregnant she had to leave college. I don't want that for you. I want you in control. I want to be able to leave what I have behind with you and feel that I've made a smart decision."

I was thinking that this conversation was crazy—my mom and I don't talk about serious things like that. But I was happy because he really cared. "Don't worry," I said. "I won't mess up, for your sake and mine."

I love my dad. He means so much to me and I wouldn't trade him for the world, not even for multi-billionaire Bill Gates. Am I still mad at him for being in jail instead of with me all those years? Yes and no. I'm mad at the decisions he made that landed him in jail, because if he hadn't gone there I would have had him in my childhood.

But maybe he needed to make the mistakes he made so he could learn from them. Besides, I'm not sure we'd be this close now if I'd known him my whole life. I'm still a little mad, but I do forgive him.

I'm glad I've been able to let go of most of my anger towards my dad. It allowed us to have a strong relationship, and it allowed me to see him as a man, not an ex-convict. It helped me learn to respect men.

It also taught me how to forgive other people in my life. I used to hold onto grudges. But after seeing what came out of forgiving my father, I've learned how to let go of my anger toward other people, too.

This year I started college in Maine, and my father is moving to Georgia to go into the real estate business. Our plan is for me to join him in Georgia after college and hopefully become his business partner one day. I just want to be close to him and if that means moving to Georgia and working with him, then so be it. We've got each other now and we're not letting go.

Dorena was 18 when she wrote this story.

What Makes a Father?

By Youth Communication

When your father is incarcerated, it's normal to feel conflicted about his role in your life. Dr. Neil Altman is a therapist and author of the book *The Analyst in the Inner City: Race, Class, and Culture Through a Psychoanalytic Lens.* He talked to us about what good fathers give, how fatherless teenagers can get those things from other people, and tips for preparing to reunite with an absent father.

Q: What does a good father give boys?

A: If you're a boy, then a father has a special role in shaping your sense of what it means to be a man. Ideas of manhood are changing, but there are still expectations that boys and men will be less emotional and more tough.

Having an older man you respect in your life, even if he's

not your dad, is important because he brings those expectations of manhood down to human size. This real man shows you that nobody can be perfectly tough or unemotional. You learn from the cracks in his façade. Seeing a father or mentor react to an emotional challenge in a good way just one time can teach a kid something.

Q: What does a good fathers give girls?

A: For girls, fathers are particularly important in adolescence. Sometimes a father and daughter who've been close when she was younger will retreat from each other when she hits puberty. Girls often feel awkward around all older men as their bodies change.

The culture is so focused on young females as sex objects that it's just as important for the girl as for the boy to get a positive male role model at that point—one who sees women as people. A girl needs to have a model of males in her life who are interested in her as a thinking and feeling person.

Q: Where can you find role models if your father is not around?

A: Seek out environments that help you develop yourself, and you'll find people who can show you the things you need. A church, for example, is both a community center and a bunch of caring people. Go where you can use any special talent you have, like making art or doing sports. Sports can help you grow because you have to cope with losing, which makes it an emotional outlet. Music is another great way of connecting to feelings.

You'll find mentors and role models in those environments where you can express emotion. And an adult you talk to but don't live with can provide you with a calmer place, a different point of view, someone to talk to who won't throw what you told them back in your face 24/7. These are some of the same things a father provides in a traditional household where the mother is with the children a lot more.

Q: How can you prepare for meeting a father who's been gone a long time?

A: Read *Dreams From My Father* by Barack Obama! Notice how Obama pays attention to the conflicting things he feels when he meets his father for the first time, and how he sorts all that out (see pp. 63-70 in the paperback). Understand that your father feels guilty and that you're going to feel angry and hopeful. There's going to be love or potential love on both sides, but you can't make the guilt and anger go away.

> **People develop fantasies of absent parents, but what you'll get is a complicated human with problems as well as some good qualities.**

Your father may want you to understand why he wasn't there for you. You won't feel understanding at first—that will have to evolve over time. But don't tell him everything you need at that first meeting. I think it's best at an initial meeting to be low-key and just find out how each other is feeling.

Talk to someone else about your feelings at first. Process that first meeting with that trusted person. Your father feels vulnerable and guilty and ashamed and worries he'll be misunderstood; he's probably not ready to hear your feelings. (It's OK if your feelings do slip out though.) After two or three meetings, you could maybe bring up some of your own feelings.

But first, you, the son or daughter, have to admit to yourself what you need from him. You're probably thinking, "I don't need him," because that's how you've coped with his absence.

Q: How do you know what you need from him if you've never had it?

A: There are clues to what you need in what you've been trying to get. As a boy, have you been drawn to gangs? To older guys who seem confident and tough? As a girl, have you been attracted to older guys of a particular type, maybe who have money? If you've been looking for it in positive places—meaning people who care about you and are reliable—that's great, that means you're more comfortable with needing it.

If you don't believe you can ever get that kind of positive attention, then your longing for it gets a little twisted. You could end up denying you need anything while seeking it out at the same time.

Q: What do you need to watch out for if you've reunited with your dad?

A: You need to find out something about your father, and the older you are, the easier this gets. What's his life like? Why does he want to see you now? Can you figure that out when you talk to him? Does he seem more mature now than he did when you were little? Is he feeling so guilty and defensive that he won't be able to handle it when you start to tell him you've been hurt and angry?

Meanwhile the people who have taken care of you—foster parents, a mother or other relative—have let you down in small ways, restricted your movements, and made you angry. You may be tempted to defy whoever's been taking care of you and think, "My father's going to swoop down and take me to a better life."

People can grow and change, even in jail. Don't assume you know what you're going to find.

People develop fantasies of absent parents. You may be expecting somebody wonderful, but what you'll get is a complicated human with lots of problems as well as some good qualities.

Q: How does jail change people?

A: People can grow and change, even in jail. Don't assume you know what you're going to find. Some people find themselves in jail; others get more bitter and hard. You have to keep your eyes open. Try to think of your father as a person, notice as much as you can. That's why I'm telling everyone to read Obama's book.

Q: Is there anything else you'd say to people who grew up without fathers?

A: I think kids who are without their biological parents—both mothers and fathers—are prone to thinking that if only they had them they would be OK. And that's not true. Biological parents come with all kinds of problems, and yes, they help, but it's not a dealbreaker for your life if you don't have them.

Part II: Parents

Back in Touch After 14 Years

By Eric Benson

I felt extremely bad about myself as a parent when I came to prison. As a teenager, I had really wanted a son. Once he was finally born, I was arrested and left him. Now, 14 years later, I still regret every day that I am not the parent that my son needed.

I have a few good memories of my son. When I held him he would stop crying. I loved the way he drooled when I took his bottle out of his mouth. I also remember taking him to a carnival in Virginia, not long before I got locked up.

I was arrested when I was 20 and my son was just 4 months old.

I'd left him home with his mother that day. I pulled out of the driveway with two friends in the car and drove for just half a block when the police came toward me in their car, head on. There were police in the car behind me, too. When I stopped, they jumped out with their guns drawn. I pictured my son's face at that moment. I had a really bad feeling. I knew my past was about to catch up with me.

I was sent to prison. Soon his mother and I broke up, and she decided that it was best that my son and I not have a relationship while I was in prison. I begged to differ. I stayed persistent year after year, writing to her, attempting to establish a relationship with my son. I never would've imagined that our separation would last for more than 14 years.

In prison I began to transform my life. I looked at my past mistakes and told myself that I was going to mature into a man and a responsible father. I dedicated myself to becoming educated and growing up so that, when given the opportunity, I could be the parent that my son deserved. Other prisoners often tell me that I have been handling my situation the right way. Their words of encouragement help me to persevere.

That first visit with my son was like an out-of-body experience.

At last, my persistence in trying to communicate with my son paid off. Not long ago, my son's mother finally allowed him to come visit me. It was the first time since he was an infant that I'd ever held or hugged my son.

That first visit was like an out-of-body experience. I was at work and the correctional officer called me and said, "You have a first-time visitor. Do you want to go on the visit?" He didn't tell me who it was, and I was curious to know who might be coming to see me for the first time when I'd been locked up for more than 14 years. "Of course I want my visit," I said.

In the visiting room, the officer told me, "Your visitors are in Row 4, Table 6." I didn't recognize the first man at the table, my son's uncle. Then I saw my son sitting with his head down on the table. Somehow, I recognized him immediately. My son is 6' 2" and has short hair like me. His bone structure is so similar to mine. He has big dark brown eyes and a familiar blush. Our baby pictures look just alike.

I was extremely happy and stunned, but I still found the voice to say, "How's everything with you, Kharon?"

"I'm OK," he said.

I asked him, "Can I have a hug?" He gave me a hug and we sat down.

"Kharon, how are you feeling right now?" I asked.

"Shocked to see you," he said.

I told him, "Everything is going to be all right."

I had so much I wanted to tell him. I started from the beginning, from when I left him as a baby. Time wouldn't allow me to express everything that I wanted to say on that day, however. When I returned to my cell I wrote him a long letter to say more about things we hadn't had time to talk about.

I stayed up for most of that night thinking about our visit and how my son looked so much like me. I cried tears of joy for finally being able to look my son in the face and hug him after so long. My heart was swollen with happiness.

On our second visit, we were communicating like close friends. I was surprised that he seemed to talk to me about any and everything. He didn't hold back.

He even talked to me about girls—I couldn't believe that! He also asked me where he'd gotten his height from, because he's taller than both his mother and me. I couldn't really answer that. Then he said, "You look just like me!" I said, "No, you look like me."

I dedicated myself to becoming educated and growing up so I could be the parent that my son deserved.

I asked him to write all of his questions down. His letter made me so happy. He had quite a few questions for me, like: "What is your favorite color? What sports did you like to play when you were younger? Were you ever an 'A' student in school? Were you ever a ladies' man?" That last question threw me for a loop.

Wish You Were Here

He said he didn't want to O.D. with the questions, but I didn't mind. I'd been waiting for the opportunity to communicate and establish a relationship with my son. I was happy to see him opening up to me in such a short time.

Since our first visit, I've been able to see my son once a month through an organization that helps incarcerated parents and their children. I'm feeling really good about how Kharon and I are getting to know each other. I can see us building a beautiful father-and-son relationship.

But I also worry about my son. I see how he holds the same materialistic mindset that I had as a teenager. That mindset hurt me in my life, and I am scared of the influence the streets can have on a materialistic 15-year-old. Will it affect my son as negatively as it affected me?

Going to parenting class helped. I learned about teenagers' typical behaviors, and I hope what I learned will help me steer my son the right way as I get to know him better. I talk to my son a lot about growing up and taking on the responsibilities of adulthood, and about being able to respect himself first before thinking about others respecting him. I want him to understand that the decisions that he makes now will affect his future.

At the end of the parenting class, I was privileged to have my son at my graduation. I gave a speech about my quest to establish a relationship with him. I was the happiest father on the planet that day. When I finished my speech, Kharon came up to the podium and gave me the biggest hug a son could give his father.

It has been more than nine months since my son and I got back in contact. I hope and pray that all goes well with my son while I continue my journey in prison, due to the bad decisions that I made when I was not much older than Kharon is now.

Eric wrote this story for Rise, *a magazine by and for parents affected by the child welfare system. Reprinted with permission. www.risemagazine.org.*

Getting Arrested Saved My Life

By Sandra Jimenez

One morning I woke up dope sick. I needed a bag of heroin. So I got up and went to a dope dealer I knew and told him I was sick and to help me out with a bag. He said to me, "Here, do this bag and sell these bags for me 'cause my brother's not here to sell for me today."

I went in the bathroom and got my fix. That day the dope was very strong 'cause he had just made a fresh batch, so I came out of that bathroom real high. I could barely see straight. I remember the dealer said to me, "Look how high and thin you look. You're a mess and even if I lose the hundred dollars, I hope the cops arrest you so you can get help, 'cause I know you're better than this."

I had never sold dope on the streets before, but it took only one time to get caught. This guy who I bought dope from every day came up to me. I said, "Yo, watsup, baby?" He said, "I'm really sick. Do you have anything on you?" I said, "Sure, how many you want?" He said, "Let me get two bags." I gave him the two bags and he gave me a twenty-dollar bill. I put it in my pocket.

Everything that happened next seemed surreal, like a movie in slow motion. I was walking towards this girl who was annoying the hell out of me, being loud, attracting attention to the corner, getting it hot. I was ready to whip her ass when something told me to look back. When I did, I saw cop cars making U turns, tires screeching, cops running towards me out of nowhere.

When I got arrested, it was like God smacked me on the head, sat me down long enough to get me sober, and made me take a look at my life.

All I could think to do was to take the eight bags of heroin I had in my hand and swallow them so the cops couldn't find them. Then they caught up to me, slammed me up against a fence, and a female cop searched my pockets. She produced a marked twenty-dollar bill. I was like, "Oh, no! This cat set me up. I'm gonna break his legs when I get out."

But you know what? What that cat did to me saved my life.

The police van was going around and around for hours all throughout the neighborhood making other busts. I guess it was sweep day. People were talking to me and all I could see was their mouths moving with no sound coming out because the heroin from the eight bags was leaking into my system. My thoughts were spinning and all I could think was, "I'm gonna die, I'm gonna die."

I started to see the people standing on corners, how obvious they looked to be selling or buying drugs. The day suddenly looked very drab and cloudy. And it smelled like death, like depression, like hell.

Finally I got to central booking, to the bullpens. I had never been in a bullpen. I had only seen them on TV. There must have been 15 women in one pen that was really made for no more than four. I finally told someone about the heroin I had swallowed and they were like, "Yo, throw up. Go to the bathroom." They weren't concerned I was going to die. No, they wanted to use the heroin I had swallowed themselves.

I was like, "These addicts are crazy." But you know what, so was I. I wanted to think I was better than them, but I was an addict, too.

The next day I went before a judge. Now let me tell you, I was at least 30 pounds underweight for my height, my hair looked crazy, I had two pairs of pants on thinking it would make me look fatter, my cheeks were sunken in. I always looked like I was whistling. I looked smoked out 'cause, oh yeah, I had a crack and alcohol problem, too.

When I looked up, who was sitting on the bench but a judge who used to be my co-worker. Yes, I used to work in the courts. Yes, I used to have a good job, a business, a marriage, a family, friends, I was well liked and I blew it all without even realizing it.

When that judge saw me, she had to take off her glasses and take a second look. She said, "Sandra?" in disbelief. Let me tell you, I wanted the earth to open up and swallow me. I had never ever felt so much shame. All I could do was put my head down and I couldn't bring myself to look up throughout the whole arraignment. She remanded me to Rikers Island and set bail.

By this time I was really high because the heroin that was double-sealed in plastic had been leaking slowly into my system. At that time, I was glad I was high because I didn't really want to face what was happening to me. There was no way I wanted to think about what I had done to my own life, or what I had done to my children. My emotions were numb, medicated.

Later on I found out that is the reason why I and many people use—so we don't have to feel, so we don't have to remember, 'cause we can't cope with the pain and memories. I sat in jail for about four days, still high, until they finally detoxed me with methadone. I called my lawyer, and she told me that the judge told her who I was, and that she knew me to be a good person, a good mother, a good co-worker, and that she didn't understand what had happened to me but that she was to help me as much as she could. She said the judge said to tell me she loved me and that she was praying for me.

That was it. I broke down and all I could do was cry and cry, a deep cry that came from deep within my soul. I cried out to God and asked him to help me, that I couldn't stand myself any more and I couldn't stop using by myself. I called my family to let them know where I was. They wanted to bail me out immediately and I said no, this is for me, I need to learn how to stay sober.

In jail, I was surrounded by all these women, hard-core institutionalized women who didn't care about life anymore. If they saw someone slit your throat or rape you, they didn't care and they wouldn't tell. I also saw women who weren't hardened yet, who had just been sentenced. They came back from court wailing, crying in despair because the judge had just given them 10 years, 15 years, 25 to life.

There was this 17-year-old in jail. She was beautiful, looked like she belonged in a magazine. She had a beautiful voice. She was intelligent, articulate. The judge gave her 25 to life for slitting a cab driver's throat. She kept saying her friend did it and asked her to take the fall because she was a minor and she would get off easy. But she was wrong.

I watched all those wasted lives, so much potential locked behind those cold bars now surrounded by cold hearts, the blank faces still asking themselves, "How did I get here?" Some contemplating suicide. Some attempting suicide. Oh yeah, that seemed like a daily thing. And I started to see myself like that, a waste, a loser, just like everybody there. And I said, "No. I will be somebody 'cause God don't make no junk."

It's one thing to talk the talk and another to walk the walk. But I was determined. Before I got arrested, my family told me I needed a program. The social workers told me I needed a program, and all I would say was, "I'm not locking myself up in no program. I don't need a program."

But when I got arrested, it was like God smacked me on the head, sat me down long enough to get me sober, and made me take a look at my life long enough to ask myself: "What am I doing? What the heck is wrong with me?"

I had to accept that by living the life I was living, I hurt not only myself, but my children and my family.

I was sent to a drug-rehabilitation program where I stayed for 17 months, living with 192 other people. I knew rehab was where I needed to be. I knew I couldn't do it alone. I was ready to surrender.

The experience of rehab was rough. If you acted out or had an attitude, you were put on Learning Experience and had to get up at 4 a.m. to brush the baseboards with a toothbrush or clean the smelly grease pits or other creative tasks. Or you had to wear costumes and signs saying what you did wrong.

One of the residents was deemed a mama's boy and they made him walk around with a diaper, a bib, a baby's bonnet and a pacifier for a few months. Sometimes people yelled in your face, screaming what they didn't like about you.

Still, I'm grateful for that experience. It let me know my character flaws in a non-sugarcoated, in-your-face way. Of course deep down inside I knew what my character defects were, but the fact that other people noticed them, too, broke down my pride, my attitude and my image. It stopped me from saying, "I'm all that," and denying the problems I had.

And in rehab, I also began connecting to the emotions that

might have led me to use in the first place. I learned that I used in order to medicate pain I didn't want to feel—especially memories of growing up with my mom.

One time during group therapy, we were listening to a tape that asked us to try to remember how we felt when we were real little kids—from 1 year old to 5 years old. But after the session, I couldn't shake the feelings that had been brought up.

Five years old was not a happy time for me. I had just come to this country, leaving all the people I knew and loved back home in the Dominican Republic. I had left my dad, my grandparents, my aunts, uncles, cousins, the familiar warmth of my home, my country, its people.

I came to the U.S. to live with my mother, but she abused me. In the session, I remembered coming here and being slapped and punched for breakfast, lunch, and dinner. I remembered welts, bruises, and broken lips. I remembered incest. I remembered being immersed in a tub of very hot water.

I had a babysitter who made lousy food. I would throw it up and she would make me eat it. I remembered all that. But most of all I still felt very vividly the sorrow and the fear of being 5 years old.

For a few months I was very depressed. Nothing made me happy. Every time I saw the therapist, I would chase her down and say, "Hey Ms. Pennula, when are we going to finish the tape? When are you going to take me out of 5 years old?"

I kept going to counseling, though, and eventually I came out of that depression. Confronting my past helped me put it behind me. I learned that my past did not have to write my future. I could break the cycle. First I had to learn not to abuse myself. Then I had to accept that by living the life I was living, I hurt not only myself, but my children and my family. 'Cause you don't live in a void. Everything you do affects somebody else.

I had seven kids when I was younger. Some live with my mother and some live with my father because when I was using drugs, I was unable to care for them. I keep in touch with them, and I have recently visited them. But I know that being without their mother all those years was hard on them. When I visited them, they told me how much they'd missed me. One day, I know I will reunite with them for good. It's my dream and my prayer.

My eighth child, my daughter Mattie, was taken from me when she was born and put into foster care. They were talking about terminating my rights when Mattie turned 6 months old. I had been in treatment for four months, and I refused to believe that God had brought me this far to allow me to lose my daughter, so I didn't lose faith. I prayed a whole lot.

The people at the foster care agency, helped me immensely. The first day I went there, my casework supervisor, Sid, said to me as I sat there scared to death and ashamed, "Forget about what you did in the past. It's what you do from today on that counts." That started a trust, because he didn't judge me.

While I was in treatment, I kept accomplishing my goals, and every time, I would go running to my caseworker and share with her my accomplishments: completing parenting classes, completing my vocational training, getting a job, getting my apartment. And she and Sid would say, "We're so proud of you. See, you're doing it," and encourage me and help me on.

Still, reunification is never easy, especially if your child was removed at birth. My daughter had become accustomed to the ways of her foster mom, and she didn't always want to be with me. The hardest times were on weekend visits. She would come home with me and she would cry for her foster mom all the time. I would wonder if it would always be this way.

But I kept going to my visits and bonding with my daughter. And, on September 18, 1998, my daughter was returned to me and the termination of parental rights case was withdrawn.

My daughter and I have our conflicts. Her foster mother was much more lenient with her than I am, so she doesn't like to be told no, even though she's only 3 years old.

Still, I'm happy to say things have gotten easier. After she had been living with me again for a couple of months, we went to an agency Christmas party. It was time to go and her foster mother said to me, "Don't let Mattie see me leave so she won't cry." So I told her, "It's all right, she won't have a problem leaving with me." After I said it, I just hoped that it was true.

> **I learned that my past did not have to write my future. I could break the cycle.**

I hailed a cab and Mattie said good-bye to her old foster mother. She didn't cry, and I guess at that point I felt she knew I was her mother and she was going to be OK with me.

From time to time I still bring my daughter to visit her foster mother because I respect the fact that to my daughter, that is also her family. But now every night when I get home from work, I feed her and get us ready for bed. Then I'll put her in my bed and read to her a picture book and explain to her what the pictures are and what the colors are and ask her questions to see if she understands. I continue to read until she falls asleep. Right now we're reading *Children's Bible Stories,* and we love it.

After I got Mattie back, I also became a parent advocate at the foster care agency. That means I helped other parents who were in the same situation I was in. Later I became the family services coordinator, supervising the parent advocates. Now I am special assistant to the executive offices, where I work on special projects. I try to help families connect to resources in their own communities, and coordinate workshops and trainings for staff and parents.

I have found a direction and a passion for helping others who are in the situation I was in, helping them see that there is a way out.

I used to ask God why he kept me alive. But now I think that if I hadn't gone through all I've been through, I wouldn't understand to the extent that I do to be able to reach out and help others, to tell them to not be too proud to ask for help. I'm not proud of some of the things I've done. But I'm willing to risk the shame to share this with others if it will help them not walk a mile in my shoes.

Sandra wrote this story in a parents' workshop at **Represent**, *a magazine for youth in foster care.*

Dreams for My Daughter

By Roger Griffin

Being a parent is probably the most difficult job in the world. You're almost always second guessing yourself, wondering if you're doing this and that right. Being a parent in prison is even more confusing. You rarely get to see your child, so it's hard to build a relationship, and you feel a heavy burden of guilt.

I was incarcerated before my daughter was born, so I didn't get to witness the joy on my girlfriend's face after the delivery. I didn't cut the umbilical cord and I wasn't there the first day they brought Aliyah home. It's hard to appreciate fatherhood, not being able to witness Aliyah's "first times." I especially wish I'd heard her first words and seen her first steps.

I'm more fortunate than other prisoners, though, because I see my daughter about once a month, talk to her several times a month, and get a letter once a week. I know people in prison with me who haven't seen their kids since they got locked up, and some of them have been in prison for 15 to 20 years.

Visits are tough. I'm in a prison in upstate New York. They start letting visitors in at 9 a.m. Family members who live in New York City have to get on the bus or start driving at about 11:00 the night before to get here that early. The prisoners don't start getting called down to the visit floor until about 10 a.m. The anticipation I feel walking to the visit floor is indescribable. Visits are the only time I really get to let my guard down in here.

The visit floor is large. There's an area for the vending machines, where you order food, snacks, and drinks. There's an area where you can take pictures with your family, and there's even a backyard area where you can go outside in good weather.

It's hard explaining to a 3-year-old that you made a mistake before she was born and are still paying for that mistake.

The playroom for the children has various toys, games, and movies. This area is rarely crowded, though, because most of the kids haven't seen their fathers, brother, or uncles in so long that they just want to spend the few hours they have sitting by them. My visits with my girlfriend and my daughter are bittersweet. I'm happy to see my family, and our visits are good, but it hurts when they leave. Time flies because there's so much to talk about in so little time.

Our best visits were Aliyah's first birthday, when I was able to see her walk and talk for the first time, and Father's Day in 2004, when Aliyah was able to talk clearly and we had a small conversation. Our most recent visit was the most painful. When she was leaving, Aliyah turned around, ran back to me, and started crying, finally asking, "Why can't you come home with me?" It's hard explaining to a 3-year-old that you made a mistake before she was born and are still paying for that mistake. So all I told her was, "Don't worry. I'll be home soon."

My nieces and nephews also ask me to come home constantly. I tell them the truth about what I did, because they're older. They were already in school when I got locked up, and they understand what prison is and why some people come here.

At the end of each visit, all of the prisoners get strip searched and then wait to go back to our housing unit. While we're waiting, we talk to each other about our families and the problems we're going through. Some are stressed after a visit because those couple of hours feel like a tease. I've seen fathers break down mentally and emotionally because they've been separated from their families for so long.

The hardest times in prison are holidays and birthdays. Because of the limited resources we have, we have to be creative with the cards we make and the poems and letters we write. Some don't get a visit on the holiday, so the closest we get to home is a phone call.

> **How can we really expect our children to look up to us when we are caged like animals?**

I associate with the prisoners who stay positive about their situations, hoping to keep a positive attitude about the situation I'm going through. Being locked up going on four years, I've learned a lot about prison and its effects on prisoners and everyone in their lives. The saying is, "We don't do prison bids by ourselves." ("Bids" are our sentences.)

Mothers become single parents, and because we're in here their responsibilities increase. Plus a lot of men in prison expect their wives or girlfriends to take care of them. I've noticed that when a prisoner is stressed, his family is also. Relationships become filled with tension and families break up. Children have no father figure to look up to and to help their mothers. How can we really expect our children to look up to us when we are caged like animals?

Sometimes I sit in my cell and thank God that I will make it home and be part of my daughter's life someday soon. A lot of the prisoners around me will never go home. I respect them because they still move forward mentally when they are forced to stand still physically.

Like any other parent, I have a lot of hopes and dreams for my daughter. I plan on spending as much time as possible with my daughter when I get out, so I can instill in her the characteristics of a leader and righteous person. I plan to spend time with my girlfriend, too, so we can get to know the new us.

I hope to witness my daughter growing into a mature and successful adult. I will tell her about the mistake I made to end up here, and stay close by her side so she doesn't grow up feeling angry and alone like I did after my mother died and I entered the foster care system.

I'm in prison, but I don't expect my daughter to grow up to be a prisoner. My hopes and dreams for my daughter and for my own life remain high.

Roger wrote this story for Rise, *a magazine by and for parents affected by the child welfare system. Reprinted with permission. www.risemagazine.org.*

Bonding from Behind Bars

By Joanne Carroll

For several years I have been facilitating the "Foster Care and Child Custody" workshop at Bedford Hills Correctional Facility in upstate New York, where I've been an inmate since 2001.

Many parents in prison whose children are in foster care are at risk of losing their rights permanently because of The Adoption and Safe Families Act (AFSA), a federal law that requires agencies to file to terminate parents' rights if their children have been in care for more than 15 of 22 months. In our group we encourage each other to stay connected to our children and fight for our parental rights.

Mothers tell their stories of how their children entered into foster care. Often drugs played a major role. Once the moms become incarcerated and the drugs leave their system, they begin to see the impact of their choices on their lives and their children's lives. Unfortunately, ASFA's 15-month clock has already begun its countdown.

There are many ways incarcerated parents can show the system that they care about their children. They can take services such as parenting classes, and pursue their GED or take college classes to show that they are striving toward self-improvement.

Parents can make their visits with their children fun by playing, reading, hugging, and kissing their children, and letting them know their mommy loves them. They can contact the foster care caseworker and ask questions about their children, like, "How is my child doing in school? Are there any behavioral issues I should know about? Do you have any suggestions that will help me to help my children through this traumatic time?"

Parenting a child from prison is challenging. But through letters, phone calls, and visits, it's possible to build a positive relationship. I tell parents, "Always do your best not to play the victim role, which upsets children who may feel abandoned by their parent. Instead, tell your children what you are doing in prison, where you work, and if you are in school."

It's important to children to stay in touch with incarcerated parents. Our children are innocent victims in our crimes.

Parenting a child from prison is challenging. But through letters, phone calls, and visits, it's possible to build a positive relationship.

When we are incarcerated, the children are traumatized. They feel abandoned. If children lose touch with their parents, they grow up wondering if their parents loved them, or why they went away.

When parents can stay in touch, children learn that what happened is not their fault, that they are loved, and that they can learn from their parent's mistakes. By being a positive role model to her children while in prison, an incarcerated mother teaches her child that if Mom can make the best out of a bad situation, they can, too.

Unfortunately, it can be very difficult for parents in prison to stay connected to their children. Parents with long sentences or who are facing TPR (termination of parental rights) can lose hope for a brighter future. They become depressed and angry at the system or themselves and lose the incentive to strive for self-improvement.

For many, the only way to stop that 15-month clock is to find a relative or friend to take their children out of the system. But as a result of drugs, or other aspects of their lifestyles prior to incarceration, many incarcerated moms have burned the bridges to their family members and don't have anyone to take their children.

When incarcerated parents stay in touch, children learn that what happened isn't their fault and that they are loved.

When it is inevitable for someone to lose her rights, we help the mother make the best possible arrangement. In general, if you make a conditional surrender agreement before TPR, and allow someone you've chosen to adopt your children, you have more control over what happens to them. You can also make a post-adoption contact agreement.

Through those agreements, a court can require the adoptive parents or a caseworker to continue to bring your children to visit you. In New York, those agreements are now court-enforceable, as long as a judge agrees that visits are in the child's best interest.

Still, in many states, contact agreements are not legally binding. Sadly, there is usually no penalty if an adoptive family does not stay in contact with the biological parent. I have seen women make an agreement, only to have contact with their child end six months later.

I am proud that my workshops are informative, and it upsets me that so many of the mothers here with children in the system have no idea what ASFA is. I wish that caseworkers and parents' attorneys would take the time to explain ASFA so parents can advocate for their families.

I also wish there were better options for all incarcerated parents—contact agreements that adoptive parents had to stick to, more adoptive parents so that children don't bounce from home to home in the system after a termination of parental rights, and exceptions to ASFA for parents in prison.

Many times parents' rights are permanently terminated even though their sentences are relatively short. I hope that caseworkers, judges and legislators can stop punishing children for their parents' crimes and find ways to help parents and children stay connected.

Joanne wrote this story for Rise, *a magazine by and for parents affected by the child welfare system. Reprinted with permission. www.risemagazine.org.*

Signing Away My Son

By Deborah McCabe

I came to court that morning with my heart and my mind racing in time with one another. I was handcuffed as we traveled from the bowels of Bronx criminal court, arriving at a phone-booth-sized room where I was told to wait for my lawyer.

It was the day for me to sign those papers.

My son, Justin, was 8 then. For the first three years of his life, Justin had slept in my bed, curled up beside me. When I got locked up, my devastation at having to leave him was palpable to anyone I came in contact with. I could not speak his name without feeling a gut-wrenching pain. Even to this day, almost 12 years later, I must mentally detach myself to cope with the pain of his absence from my life.

Five years into my sentence, I had to go to court to surrender my rights so Justin could be adopted. I still had years to go and there was no one else to take him. Besides, I felt it would have been selfish to fight. He was with a family that loved him. I grew up in foster care, so I know how rare that can be.

When I was first incarcerated, Justin's foster parents had reminded me of the unbreakable bond my son and I shared. I warned them that I wouldn't be home for a very long time. I told them to keep my son away from me. After all, he was only 3. I thought his memory of me would fade and his life might even turn out normal. Despite my protests, they allowed me to talk on the phone with Justin weekly and brought him to visit often.

Our visits during those initial years were painful but wondrous. When he saw me walk through the visiting room door, Justin would fly across the room and leap into my arms. His face would light up and he would shower my face with kisses and wipe away my tears with his little hands. Each time it seemed as if he had grown a little bit, or changed in some small, almost imperceptible way. I still remember the sound of his voice when "Mommy" changed to "Mom."

Almost 12 years later, I must mentally detach myself to cope with the pain of my son's absence from my life.

Justin and I participated in the Summer Program and Family Reunion Program (FRP) at the prison facility. God, how I lived for those visits. With the Summer Program, Justin came to see me every day for five days. During those days, our relationship blossomed into something truly untouchable.

With FRP, we were able to spend two days and nights in a trailer within the bounds of the facility. We were a real family again. One day a basketball bounced and knocked out his naturally loosened two front teeth. Another time I held his scrawny 6-year-old body in my arms and sang to him. He watched me sing so intently, staring up at me as if I was the sun, moon, and stars all rolled in one.

It was at the end of one of those trailer visits that I finally got a glimpse of all the pain my baby felt. I asked him if he was ready to go and he actually stopped being strong for me and cried. I had not seen him cry until then, almost three years after my incarceration.

But as Justin grew older, things between his foster family and me began to change. What once seemed an ideal relationship between a mother and surrogate mother slowly turned sour. I felt like his foster mother became jealous of our relationship.

Justin began missing every other visit. They made the excuse that Justin was impressionable and they didn't want him to visit prison. Then they told me that Justin had school or appointments. They didn't send him even when I arranged transportation.

On more than one occasion, Justin's foster mother told me that Justin got depressed after visits and acted out by being disrespectful or breaking his possessions. Those were little signs, she told me, that "maybe the visits aren't such a good idea." I felt that if he were allowed to see me more often, then it would not be so devastating to say goodbye. They told me they knew what was best for him and I was being selfish.

In 2001, there was an order from the court for me to attend a hearing that would determine whether I would retain my rights to my son. By then, the law had changed. Children couldn't stay in foster care for years and years. A federal law called ASFA had been passed, saying that you can't have a child in a foster placement for more than 15 out of 22 months. I had no family that could take Justin out of the system. My choices were: fight and maybe still have my rights terminated, or sign a post-adoption contact agreement and pray they'd keep bringing him to visit. I chose to sign.

During the adoption proceeding, we agreed that he would visit me seven times a year. Three visits were supposed to be trailer visits, plus I'd get phone calls, pictures, and letters. The lawyer made it sound so simple. She quickly handed me the papers to sign.

Signing Away My Son

What I didn't know was that his family would soon disregard the promises they made in court, and at that time, post-adoption contact agreements were not legally binding in New York. That meant that his adoptive family didn't have to follow through on our agreement. (These kinds of agreements are now court-enforceable in New York, though not in other states.)

I tried my best to hold my emotions in check that day, but I could feel the weight of what I was about to do bearing down on me. When I finally walked out those courtroom doors, my eyes were blinded by tears. I turned to say, "Maybe I'm not sure, maybe I'm making a mistake." My lawyer was already gone.

I felt like nothing, as if I allowed them to take away my reason for breathing. I was no longer a mother, because I no longer had the legal right to claim my own child. I was just a criminal now.

Shortly after the hearing, I realized what a mistake I had made. Justin's family stood me up for the next two visits that we had arranged. They also stopped calling. I contacted the lawyer about undoing the adoption, but she told me it was too late. She said it was up to the adoptive parents to arrange visits and that she was sorry they hadn't brought Justin. "Yeah, I'm sorry too," I said.

My son's adoptive parents don't seem to realize how much they have hurt us both by keeping us apart.

I was devastated. Visits with my son were what I looked forward to, what I lived for. How could I give up being his mommy? I became so depressed that I had to go on anti-depressants just to get myself out of bed in the morning.

I have had two visits since I signed the adoption papers five years ago. I have spoken to my son only five times on the phone. His family put a block on the phone so it couldn't accept collect calls. I offered to pay for calls but his adoptive mother wouldn't allow me to do so.

His adoptive father told me once that I shouldn't complain because I wouldn't be able to be his mother again until my release. Once they sent a letter telling me I was lucky that they didn't send him back. I remember being in foster care and being "sent back" and I hope he never knows what that feels like.

The last time I saw Justin, he was 9 years old. Two weeks ago he turned 14.

I call my son once a month. My advocate is able to place the call for me. It is rare for the woman who answers not to hang up when she hears my voice on the other end. If I am blessed to reach my son by phone, my advocate allows me extra time because she knows I only get to parent him for an about an hour each year.

I used to write him but he said he never got one letter. I used to send him things for his birthday but the store would refund my money after they sent it back.

I have two pictures of Justin, taken after the two trailers we had together. His smile is big and bright. The happiness he experienced just being with me shows. I keep a journal for him. I have made him a scrapbook. And I am faithful in disappointing myself monthly with my phone calls. I hope he feels my love.

When I do talk to Justin on the phone, I tell him to be respectful and grateful to all the people who love him. The last time I spoke to him was more than a year ago. He was turning 13. In the first few minutes of our conversation he sounded apprehensive. I reminded him that I love him and that we may not have the opportunity to speak or see each other for a while.

He tries not to hurt my feelings by speaking too fondly of his adoptive family but I want to know if he knows love and affection. At 13 he sounded like he was still a very innocent teenager, much more so than I was.

My son's adoptive parents don't seem to realize how much they have hurt us both by keeping us apart. Still, I am very grateful to his adoptive parents for loving him, taking him when there was no one else, giving him the life I couldn't give, instilling good values in him, allowing him to have a childhood, and protecting him.

I hope to have the chance to be a mom to Justin again. I might go home in 9 months or 18 months, and when I do, I hope to reestablish a relationship with my son. I believe that no matter how old you are, you always need a mother's love.

I can hear how much he misses me when I talk to him. He always asks me when I am coming for him. Justin told me that he calls the toys he received from me his "special toys." He said he doesn't play with them but saves them so they won't break. My little brother did the same thing with toys from my mom when he was in foster care.

Two years ago, my sister was allowed to see my son and made a video. In it, Justin said he loved me, missed me, and couldn't wait for me to get out. He asked if I was saving him that birthday cake he never came to get. (The Children's Center here provides cake if your child is coming for a birthday.) Mind you, it had been years since I told him about the cake. I felt like he was asking me if I still loved him and was saving my love for him.

Last time we spoke, Justin told me that he was going to arrange a way to see me the following week. I gave him numbers to call and my address, but I haven't heard from him yet.

Deborah wrote this story for Rise, *a magazine by and for parents affected by the child welfare system. Reprinted with permission. www.risemagazine.org.*

Sentenced to Be Alone

By Natasha Santos

In the foster care system, many of us have to deal with the fact that we are away from our biological parents. We often have to squeeze in our hugs and kisses in the one to three hours that we have been given for visits, and make do with that until we see them again.

When a parent is in prison, maintaining a connection can be even harder. For example, when parents are sent to jail in rural counties far away from the inner cities where their children live, it puts strain on their relationships with their kids and their families. Many teens feel abandoned and many kids feel confused about why Mommy or Daddy is stuck behind that glass wall.

We interviewed Nell Bernstein, the author of *All Alone in the World*, a book about the effects that the arrest and imprisonment of parents has on children. She points out that current policies work to keep parents in prison apart from their children, even though it's been shown that maintaining parent-child relationships helps incarcerated parents turn their lives around and makes it less likely that their kids will get into trouble. Bernstein investigates why this is, and tells us what can be done about it.

Q: How do prison policies work to break up families?

A: Incarcerated parents are an average of 150 miles from their children. Most prisoners come from the densely populated urban areas—like New York City—but are sent to prisons in rural areas. When the Osborne Association, an advocacy group for children of incarcerated parents, takes kids to visit their parents once a year, they take them on a plane.

Hawaii puts their prisoners in private prisons on the mainland, because it's very expensive to bring food and supplies to an island. So those parents never see their kids.

We're a country that preaches family values, and yet we have policies that forcibly separate families. As of 2007, about 1.7 million kids had an incarcerated parent—that's almost 3 out of every 100 children. And minorities suffer more than whites: an African-American child is nine times more likely than a white child to have their parent incarcerated.

Q: How does it affect children when they are not able to visit their parents?

A: Each child is different, but the main thing I learned is that the loss feels the same—just like if I wasn't able to see my kid for years and years. The main harm is just loss, because kids need their parents.

Then there's the stigma—some kids feel ashamed and feel they need to keep it secret, and sometimes the family keeps it secret from the kids. They tell them their father is in the military, or mom went off to college. So then the kids become part of this family charade.

Only a small percentage of parents who are incarcerated have their kids go into foster care. But no matter what, it's still really hard to reconnect once the parent returns home. There's often a lot of tension. Parents often want to exercise authority because they've never been able to before, and the kids don't really want to hear it.

Q: Why should prisoners have access to their kids?

A: To me it's more about why kids should have access to their parents. Any benefit that we think family has for kids, a family with the parent in jail has, too. I know it sounds corny, but love is really in short supply. And kids need it. We shouldn't block them from getting it from parents they have who are in prison.

It's been shown that seeing their families makes prisoners less likely to go back to prison after they get out.

I met some incarcerated parents who thought they were protecting their kids by not having them come to visit, because prison is not a pleasant place. But many kids feel rejected by that. They actually feel better knowing that their parents want them and their parent is safe.

It's also been shown that seeing their families makes prisoners less likely to go back to prison after they get out. A warden told me that any good warden knows that family visits are one of the best things you can have.

Q: Do all state policies tend to break up families or do some work differently?

A: A few states, like Oregon, have overhauled their prison system to take family connections into account. We're also seeing more and more forward thinking by people in state government and by administrators who realize that it is more humane and good policy to recognize and support family connections.

Some states have policies that are supposed to keep children in touch with the parents when they are incarcerated, and they have model programs. But it can be pretty complex to get a visit, and many kids fall through the cracks.

The perception among politicians is that people think prisoners *should* have their kids taken away. Public opinion is shifting, but politicians are still behind. One politician told me that he felt he could now vote against new "tough on crime" laws, but was still scared to vote to get rid of the laws that already exist.

Q: What recommendations do you have to improve the system for the children of parents in prison?

A: The only reason I can presume to make recommendations as a journalist is they're all based on what the children I interviewed told me. All the policy suggestions really come directly from the young people.

The overall idea is that children have to be visible and cared for in every part of the criminal justice system, from the parent's arrest all the way through. If the police don't have to break the door down, don't. If you don't have to handcuff a mother in front of her kids, don't do it. If visiting hours can be extended, and waiting rooms made more child-friendly, they should be.

At the San Francisco Partnership for Incarcerated Parents, we're working on something called the Bill of Rights for Children of Incarcerated Parents. It's a bill that states eight rights of children with parents in jail, including the right to see their parents, the right to be well cared for, the right to be heard when decisions are made about them, and the right to be considered when decisions are made about their parent. We're working with our local government in San Francisco to make it happen, and there are now about 15 other sites that are launching campaigns around the Bill of Rights.

> *Just because your parent makes a mistakes doesn't mean you should not be able to see them.*

Q: What needs to be done for the parents so they can stay connected with their kids when they get out?

A: We have to get rid of the laws that make it impossible to make a living and be there for your kids when you get out of prison. In the '90s we passed laws saying you can't live in public housing or get public assistance if you've been to prison. Sometimes kids move in with a relative in public housing, and their parent literally can't visit them because they're worried about getting the relative kicked out of public housing.

In San Francisco they have recruiting posters for foster parents that say, "You don't have to be perfect to be a parent." And it's kind of ironic. We don't ask foster parents to be perfect. But if biological parents screw up and get convicted of a crime, they can lose contact with their kids. But I really think that slogan is true. Just because your parent makes a mistakes doesn't mean you should not be able to see them.

Natasha was 18 when she wrote this story. She went to college and worked as an advocate for youth in foster care.

Special Delivery

By Derrick Alexander

Celebrating holidays and birthdays with my family has always been important to me. When I was a child, my parents were able to make our special occasions memorable.

One Christmas, my parents played a trick on my sister and me. My mom and dad acted as though we wouldn't be able to exchange too many gifts that year. I scouted the house to find gifts hidden away but couldn't find any. My sister and I prepared ourselves for a meager celebration.

On Christmas morning, when I peeked under the tree, it seemed rather bare. Mom and Dad acted unenthusiastic—until my dad slipped away and returned with many unexpected gifts: a bike, a video game, clothes, games, and shoes. My sister and I were so shocked and surprised and appreciated our gifts even more.

My wife and I actually replayed that special moment with

our own two daughters. My children shared the same sparkle in their eyes I'd had as a child. I was definitely a proud father at that moment.

Now that I'm incarcerated, though, holidays are difficult moments for my family and me. My wife and children live down south now and can't visit me in upstate New York too often.

As I prepare for the holidays without them, I feel a great sadness and enter a period of stagnation and depression. The contrast between what I could have at home and the activities my current environment has to offer is painful. I know my family suffers, too. A missing parent severely dampens the fun of birthdays and holidays.

I try to use my time in prison to mature and grow so I can be a better father.

I very much appreciate the occasional visit I have with my family, although they end with a bit of depression for us all because they remind us of our separation. I try not to let my spirits stay down for long, and I try to use my time in prison to mature and grow so I can be a better father.

In the long months between visits, we stay close by mail. I am a bit of an artist so I try to express my love and commitment to my family through my work. I write my children encouraging letters decorated with pictures related to my topic. I take great care with my cartoons and drawings, and my daughters seem to truly enjoy our correspondence. My letters have even encouraged them to write and send their artwork to me.

It lifts my spirits when my children express themselves to me through their artwork. I see them following in my footsteps in a positive way. Although my imprisonment has impacted us all, I'm proud that we've found a way to express our love and commitment and to keep ourselves optimistic.

Derrick wrote this story for Rise, *a magazine by and for parents affected by the child welfare system. Reprinted with permission. www.risemagazine.org.*

I Lost My Rights But Not My Girls

By Bliss Edwards

After I'd been in prison for two years, my two daughters were placed in foster care. They had been shifting back and forth between my aunt and sister. My aunt suffered from some medical issues and my sister had three children of her own. Eventually, they could no longer take care of my daughters, especially since I still had nine years to do. They contacted social services because we had no other family to take the girls.

Once the child welfare system got involved, I was so stressed out. My girls were shipped around and split up. I wasn't allowed to have their addresses or phone numbers. I was also served with court papers stating I had 15 months to get my children out of foster care or else I would be charged with neglect and would permanently lose my rights.

There was nothing I could do. I had no family or friends who could take them and I had time to do. My heart was broken and I felt helpless.

I kept going back and forth to court, hoping for a miracle. I dragged out my court case for almost a year. Unfortunately, I was stuck between having my rights taken away or voluntarily giving up my rights with conditions. I felt like my world was crumbling and I was defeated.

> **I had no family or friends who could take in my daughters, and I had time to do. I felt helpless.**

I decided to give up my rights with the condition that my sister or their father still would be able to bring them to visit me. Unfortunately, my sister got ill and their father has not come. However, I have been fortunate enough to continue seeing my children. The caseworker arranged it so that if I call and schedule a visit, she will bring them once a month for an hour. Although an hour is not much time it is better than not seeing them at all.

It is important to never give up hope and to take advantage of every opportunity. I make the best out of that one hour a month and I maintain my relationship with my daughters through the mail. I want my children to know I love them. I also want to teach them to be the best that they can be.

I hope that, although I've lost my rights, we will never be too old to be a family together. I will never give up hope or the fight to see and know my two beautiful daughters.

This story was originally published in Rise, *a magazine by and for parents affected by the child welfare system, www.risemagazine.org.*

Paying the Price

By Ayinde Fair

July 4, 2004 was one of the best days of my life. I was sitting in a cell in a prison in upstate New York, thinking about all the things I'd been through in the past five years. It was a hot summer day and all of my friends were going on visits. I was thinking, "Man, I need a visit." I was stressed out.

Around 9:15 the officer announced, "Inmate Fair, you have a visit." I couldn't believe it. At that time, I had been in prison for three years. I was far from my family in Queens and only received visits once in a while.

As I got ready I thought, "Who is coming to see me? More than likely it's my mother. She always comes through for me when I least expect it."

When I got to the visiting area, I saw my family sitting at a table. My mother had a funny look on her face. When I got to the table, I almost fell out. I was looking into the eyes of my beautiful daughter, Brittany. I hadn't seen my daughter for five years—since she was 2 years old.

I thought, "She looks just like her mother, with a little resemblance to me." Brittany had her hair in cornrows and a beautiful smile on her face. She was small, and I was sure she was going to be short because her mother is only 4 feet 11 inches.

My mother often visited my daughter, who lived with an aunt. She always told me how Brittany was doing. My mother said that Brittany acts like me and was doing well in school. But Brittany's family wouldn't let her visit me.

I sat down with her and held her in my arms. I called her "Little Me." Then I picked her up and held her tight, and she wrapped her arms around me, saying, "Hi, Daddy."

Over the course of my bid (sentence), I tried to reach out to my daughter, but to no avail. Her family was giving me a hard time. When I called the house they didn't accept my call. I tried writing to my daughter and her aunt, but I didn't get any response.

I was hurting, because I knew that I'd messed up. I grew up without my father, and I knew Brittany was hurting by not having me home with her.

When my mother spent time with Brittany, she would ask to bring her up to see me, but her aunt would never give up the birth certificate so she could come. (She needed to bring identification.)

I found out later that Brittany was adopted by her aunt in 1999. Something happened with Brittany's mother—to this day I still don't know what—and she lost custody of Brittany. Her aunt adopted her so that the foster care system wouldn't take her. I was locked up on Riker's Island at the time and wasn't told what was going on. I wish the court system had done a thorough investigation to find me so I could've been a part of that decision.

Although my mother was spending time with Brittany, she was also unaware of the adoption. We both found out in

2000, after the adoption was done. (I think that's why her aunt wouldn't give the birth certificate—because it would've shown that she was adopted.)

Finally, in 2002, I got back in contact with my daughter's mother. She was always in contact with Brittany and every time she came to New York she would visit her. Brittany's mother started coming to see me a few times.

At last, my mother convinced Brittany's family to let her see me. Her mother came, too. I was so happy to see all of my family together. Brittany sat on my lap and we talked. I asked her, "Are you mad at me?" "A little bit," she told me.

I guess that, at her age, she couldn't really understand my situation. Nevertheless, I told her the truth. I said, "I made some mistakes in life and I am paying the price for them. But I'm doing everything I can to change my life and make things better for the future."

As I explained this to her, I was hurting, because I knew that I'd messed up. I grew up without my father, and I knew Brittany was hurting by not having me home with her. It hurt me, too, that we were separated for five years. I missed a lot of her childhood.

After a while, we decided to go for a walk, but Brittany wanted me to carry her. As I walked with her in my arms, I asked her about school. She told me how well she was doing and said that she would send her report card. I told her, "I'm proud of you. Keep up the good work." I explained that education is important and she should always study.

The whole visit, Brittany stayed on my lap or in my arms. It really felt good to hold my daughter. We also took pictures together, played cards, and joked around. We had fun on that day. The pictures we took were the first I'd taken, and smiled for, in years.

My mother was shocked because she had never seen Brittany be so good and seem so happy. I told my mother, "She is Daddy's little girl." I was sure she felt the positive energy and love coming from me.

At 2 p.m. our visiting time was almost up. I asked Brittany, "Do you want to come see me again?" "Yes," she said. I told her how much I loved her and that I was sorry for not being home with her. I also told her that I wanted to send her some things and asked her to let me know when she got them.

> **I get involved in every program the prison has to offer, including a fatherhood class.**

Before the visit was over, I looked at my mother and she started to cry. She had not seen me happy in so long. As we were getting ready to part, Brittany told me that she loved me and would miss me. It felt really good to hear her say that. I told her, "I will think of your every day and night, and I love you."

"Goodbye, Daddy, I will see you next time," she said.

"I can't wait," I replied, holding her tight one last time.

I went back to my cell feeling really good. I told all my friends that I'd seen my daughter. They were happy for me.

Seeing Brittany gave me extra strength to stay focused and fight harder for my freedom. I have eight years left on my sentence. If I don't win my appeal I will have to do all of that time. In the last three years, I've begun to educate myself by taking college courses in business and being involved in every program the prison has to offer me, including a fatherhood class.

In the parenting class, I learned that I really can be a father to Brittany from behind these walls. By communicating more through writing, phone calls, and visits, I can do my duty. Even if I don't always get responses, as long as I don't give up and continue to write and call, it will help our relationship grow.

Since our first visit, we have grown closer and closer. I write to her every week and I try to call at least once a week. I like to send her books and business magazines and other gifts to let her know I'm thinking of her. Our phone calls have been getting better now that she is getting older. She tells me how she is doing

Paying the Price

in school and the game systems she wants (which is mostly all of them). She tells me that most of the time she is either on the computer or studying.

Her aunt seems more accepting now. In fact, she brought Brittany up to my graduation from the parenting class. I'm not sure what's changed, because I have not talked to Brittany's aunt about what happened yet. I want to take things slow and we have not had a chance to be alone to really talk.

I love my little girl dearly and I'm very proud of Brittany. She graduated elementary school and she's off to junior high. As I've gotten to know her, I've seen that some of her ways and actions are like my own. Little things she does reminded me of myself. When she gets mad, she screws up her face and looks just like me.

I hope and pray that Brittany stays on the right track and does not hang out with the wrong people. I will be there for her to help her stay on the straight path. When she gets older, I will also tell her more about my life and the mistakes I've made. I want to make sure that she understands why I'm here.

Once I'm released, I pray that we will have a beautiful relationship. I hope that when I get myself together, Brittany can come and live with me, or at least stay for the summer or during school vacations. I plan on spending a lot of time with my little girl.

Ayinde wrote this story for Rise, *a magazine by and for parents affected by the child welfare system. Reprinted with permission. www.risemagazine.org.*

Sugar Daddy

By Jermaine Archer

It was a hot, humid July day. All the neighborhood children were outside. Teenagers were playing in the fire hydrant spray to cool off. Younger girls were jumping rope and boys were playing handball. A few young men were playing stickball in the street.

My birthday was approaching and I had gone out the day before and bought bikes for my two children, Raven and Shai. I always liked buying them presents on my birthday. I grew up poor with seven brothers, four sisters, a caring, beautiful mother and a drunk, abusive father. I vowed never to be like my father.

As soon as I was old enough, I decided to buy me a gun and some drugs to sell. At 14, it seemed only logical to me that as long as I had a gun, I would never be broke.

First I went on several unarmed robbery sprees, some of which were almost comical. Once I barely scraped by with $55

Sugar Daddy

after a hand-to-hand tussle with a brawny older guy. With my stick-up money and $50 chipped in by a friend, I bought a handgun and a couple grams of cocaine. Then, after a number of easier robberies, I had plenty of cocaine to sell. The money came fast and easy. I was living the high life.

I thought of myself as a businessman. I bought a product wholesale and sold it retail at a profit. I reasoned that, if I didn't sell it, someone else would. This was evident because of the demand for drugs in my neighborhood. I also truly believed I was doing it for my family. It never occured to me that my behavior would lead to my separation from the family I loved.

But when I had enough money to give up dealing and go legit, I didn't. Even though I'd been arrested many times and most of my original partners were either dead or serving lengthy prison sentences, I didn't want to stop dealing. I was addicted to the money and power, to seeing the looks on people's faces when I handed them presents and cash.

The neighborhood children would line up at the ice cream truck and order what they wanted when I was around. Because the parents couldn't afford it, I always paid for everybody's Klondikes and King Cones.

On this day, the ice cream truck had come and gone. All of the children, and some of the

At 14, it seemed only logical to me that as long as I had a gun, I would never be broke.

parents, were smearing their faces with ice cream. I finished my Banana Boat, went upstairs and returned with a hot pink Barbie bicycle with training wheels. Raven's eyes lit up like a sparkler and she charged me like an out of control taxi. She hugged my leg, jumped on the bike and took off with a bunch of neighborhood kids in hot pursuit.

Shai looked up at me confused: "What about me?" For him I had a black and yellow bumblebee bike. He hopped on so quickly, he nearly toppled over. I steadied him, but as he tried to take

117

off, we both realized his feet couldn't touch the pedals.

That afternoon, I just pushed him around, and after he went to bed, his uncle Mike and I readjusted the seat pole and the pedals. The next day, I felt on top of the world watching him and Raven race up and down the block, enjoying themselves.

But those days came to an end. Eventually the local police labeled me a menace to society. Soon I was targeted by many people—the police, other dealers, and stick-up kids. I thought I could protect myself and was outsmarting everyone, but my judgment had become cloudy. My future was being written by the police. Soon I got locked up for a murder that took place on a block I controlled. The police knew I either did it or allowed it to happen.

> **I also truly believed I was doing it for my family. It never occured to me that my behavior would lead to my separation from the family I loved.**

I refused to cooperate, not knowing the lengths the police and prosecutor would go to take me off the streets. Looking back, I am no longer mad at the people who orchestrated my demise. I realize that how the world perceived me was true. I was a menace.

Today, sitting in Sing Sing Correctional Facility, staring out the dirty windows at the Hudson River, I see how blind I was. I was hurting my children more than I was doing anything positive for them. I was a horrible role model for Shai. Now I am out of their lives. Their mother relocated to Connecticut and I no longer see them as often as I'd like. I write to my children, but that's not the same as being there.

One year, I saw them only twice. Raven is now 14 and Shai is 13. He made it clear that he felt abandoned by me. I missed out on their childhood years. By the time I am eligible to go home, Raven will be 28 and Shai 27, older than I was when I was arrested.

Sometimes now I look back on that day with the bicycles. My

Sugar Daddy

children were happy, their mother was happy, and I had contributed to that happiness. That's a time I'll always remember. But if I could do it all over again, I would raise my kids like my mother raised me: with more love and happiness than money and material things.

I tried to do better than my father, to give my kids what I believed I was missing. But I feel I've failed as a father. I pray that one day I can receive a second chance to connect with my children. I only hope my children can forgive me.

Jermaine wrote this story for Rise, *a magazine by and for parents affected by the child welfare system. Reprinted with permission. www.risemagazine.org.*

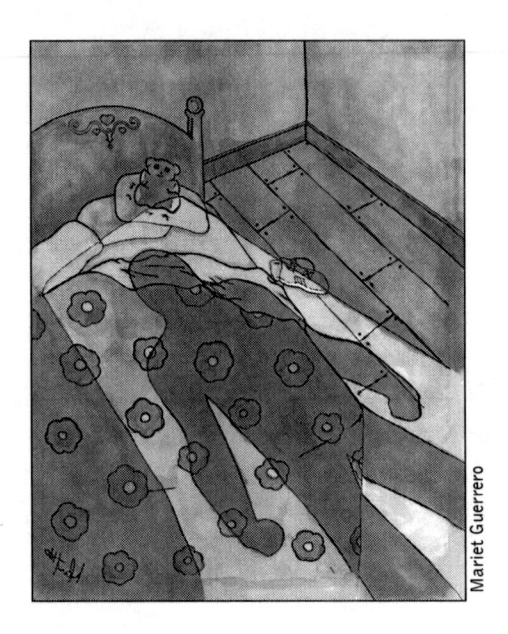

"I'm Sorry": A Sex Offender Tells His Story

By Anonymous

When I was a child, I was sexually abused by my father. I wanted his love and companionship; I just didn't want the touching. But I didn't want to lose the relationship I had with him either, so I didn't tell him to stop. Instead, I found another way to escape. When I was being abused, I would feel myself floating up to the ceiling. It let me go out of my body and detach my emotions.

I was an adult with a family of my own when I found I was fantasizing a lot about having sexual contact. But the more I thought about sex, the person became not a person, but more of an idea, just a thing to touch. I was married and I had 8 children, 5 girls and 3 boys. My children have told me that at the time I was hostile and aggressive and angry all the time. Even though there were some good times, I created an environment that was a nightmare, a terror, and they dreaded me coming home.

Then I began to sexually abuse my children and two of my daughters' girlfriends, who were around 14 or 15.

I would look in their bedroom at night to check to see if they were in bed, like I had since they were little girls, and then I'd fondle them. I would tell myself, "This is certainly something I don't want to do. I won't ever do it again."

Then I would start thinking about touching again, and I would get aroused. I realized I had a problem, but part of me just shut down and denied it. I was very scared that if I was found out I would lose my position and my family, that I would have to admit what I had done wrong to the ones I had abused.

Then one of my daughters went to her godfather and told him what had been happening. He said, "I've known Nick a long time and I don't believe he would do that. But if it's true, let's go talk to him about it." My daughter said she wanted to deal with it herself. But he said he would only give her a short time. Otherwise, his conscience and his manhood mandated that he go talk to me.

> *I realized I had a problem, but part of me just shut down and denied it.*

Eventually he asked me, "Nick, have you been sexually molesting your daughters?" And I said, "What are you talking about?" He said, "Nick, I'm sorry to have to ask you this as a friend. Have you been sexually molesting your daughters?" And I said, "Yes, I have."

It was shocking to me and it was shocking to him. We were both afraid of what might happen, that there might be a violent blow up. I suggested I call my wife and let her know what had happened, and tell her it was my fault and not the children's fault.

After that, he was supportive, understanding, firm. He didn't know if I might commit suicide. That was something I thought about myself. I thought it might be the best thing if that's what it took to make the world safe. All of my family pleaded with me and they said that whatever I had done, it would be far worse if I killed myself, because then they would have to deal with that, too.

We went to family therapy and then I turned myself into the D.A. (a government prosecutor). I said, "Here I am," and he said, "You should go talk to a lawyer." And I said, "I won't do that. I won't put myself up against my family," and I went to jail.

When I went to jail, I was shocked. There were about 100 people in my wing, and about 85 out of 100 admitted to me that they had been involved in child sexual abuse. Some were very motivated to change, very aware; some were still in denial; and some didn't think what they did was wrong. Those were the people who really horrified me.

I did want to change, and for me group therapy helped. Talking about what happened was like coming back alive again, becoming a real person rather than a fake. I was alive rather than dead and dying. I was filled with hope rather than a nightmare. I couldn't correct what had happened in the past, but I could set guidelines to prevent it in the future.

First, I had to deal with the fact that I had been abused myself. The hardest thing to accept is that it really did happen. You want to say, "No, no, no." But I couldn't heal till I had accepted that I had experienced it.

Then I needed to deal with what I had done. By sharing our stories in group therapy, we saw patterns to watch out for. For instance, if I'm in a cycle and I'm depressed and angry, and then I start drinking and drugging, and then I start fantasizing, I have to stop myself, or pick up the phone and call my therapist, or call a friend, and say, "Something is wrong."

Some of my children opted not to talk to me, and some were prevented by a restraining order. Still, I was grateful that four out of eight of them have made contact with me since that time. They've told me that they're glad I'm living honestly, they're glad

I'm in therapy.

I've done some public speaking now about being a sexual abuser and they're very supportive of that work. I think they would have been filled with hatred if I had not been honest and open. They've been to therapy too. One of them, like me, made the decision to talk openly with other people about the abuse.

When my father abused me, part of me hated him and wanted revenge, and part of me loved him. The fact that I felt love for him was incomprehensible to me. When I confronted him about the abuse, he refused to talk about it, so I had to find other ways of coming to terms with it. I had to realize that he was the person who was sick and troubled and that I didn't do anything wrong as a child. It was important to get rid of that guilt that I participated in it, even unwillingly, that I had my body react, even if I couldn't control it.

> *Talking about what happened was like coming back alive again, becoming a real person rather than a fake.*

If I had to say one thing to a victim, I would say, "I'm so sorry for what I did. Me, I did it. It's not your fault. I was the one who was wrong. Don't attack yourself. Attack what I did. I know I can never make it up to you, but I'm going to show you that I'm trying to change."

And I would say, "You need to get help for yourself, not from me, but get help. If I had gotten help earlier, I don't think I would have done as much abuse as I did."

The author shared his story through Stop It Now!, which runs the sexual abuse helpline 1-888-PREVENT.

Teens:
How to Get More Out of This Book

Self-help: The teens who wrote the stories in this book did so because they hope that telling their stories will help readers who are facing similar challenges. They want you to know that you are not alone, and that taking specific steps can help you manage or overcome very difficult situations. They've done their best to be clear about the actions that worked for them so you can see if they'll work for you.

Writing: You can also use the book to improve your writing skills. Each teen in this book wrote 5-10 drafts of his or her story before it was published. If you read the stories closely you'll see that the teens work to include a beginning, a middle, and an end, and good scenes, description, dialogue, and anecdotes (little stories). To improve your writing, take a look at how these writers construct their stories. Try some of their techniques in your own writing.

Resources on the Web

We will occasionally post Think About It questions on our website, www.youthcomm.org, to accompany stories in this and other Youth Communication books. We try out the questions with teens and post the ones they like best. Many teens report that writing answers to those questions in a journal is very helpful.

How to Use This Book in Staff Training

Staff say that reading these stories gives them greater insight into what teens are thinking and feeling, and new strategies for working with them. You can help the staff you work with by using these stories as case studies.

Select one story to read in the group, and ask staff to identify and discuss the main issue facing the teen. There may be disagreement about this, based on the background and experience of staff. That is fine. One point of the exercise is that teens have complex lives and needs. Adults can probably be more effective if they don't focus too narrowly and can see several dimensions of their clients.

Ask staff: What issues or feelings does the story provoke in them? What kind of help do they think the teen wants? What interventions are likely to be most promising? Least effective? Why? How would you build trust with the teen writer? How have other adults failed the teen, and how might that affect his or her willingness to accept help? What other resources would be helpful to this teen, such as peer support, a mentor, counseling, family therapy, etc?

Resources on the Web

From time to time we will post Think About It questions on our website, www.youthcomm.org, to accompany stories in this and other Youth Communication books. We try out the questions with teens and post the ones that they find most effective. We'll also post lessons for some of the stories. Adults can use the questions and lessons in workshops.

Using the Book

> **Discussion Guide**

Teachers and Staff:
How to Use This Book in Groups

When working with teens individually or in groups, you can use these stories to help young people face difficult issues in a way that feels safe to them. That's because talking about the issues in the stories usually feels safer to teens than talking about those same issues in their own lives. Addressing issues through the stories allows for some personal distance; they hit close to home, but not too close. Talking about them opens up a safe place for reflection. As teens gain confidence talking about the issues in the stories, they usually become more comfortable talking about those issues in their own lives.

Below are general questions to guide your discussion. In most cases you can read a story and conduct a discussion in one 45-minute session. Teens are usually happy to read the stories aloud, with each teen reading a paragraph or two. (Allow teens to pass if they don't want to read.) It takes 10-15 minutes to read a story straight through. However, it is often more effective to let workshop participants make comments and discuss the story as you go along. The workshop leader may even want to annotate her copy of the story beforehand with key questions.

If teens read the story ahead of time or silently, it's good to break the ice with a few questions that get everyone on the same page: Who is the main character? How old is she? What happened to her? How did she respond? Another good starting question is: "What stood out for you in the story?" Go around the room and let each person briefly mention one thing.

Then move on to open-ended questions, which encourage participants to think more deeply about what the writers were feeling, the choices they faced, and the actions they took. There are no right or wrong answers to the open-ended questions.

Using the Book

Open-ended questions encourage participants to think about how the themes, emotions, and choices in the stories relate to their own lives. Here are some examples of open-ended questions that we have found to be effective. You can use variations of these questions with almost any story in this book.

—What main problem or challenge did the writer face?

—What choices did the teen have in trying to deal with the problem?

—Which way of dealing with the problem was most effective for the teen? Why?

—What strengths, skills, or resources did the teen use to address the challenge?

—If you were in the writer's shoes, what would you have done?

—What could adults have done better to help this young person?

—What have you learned by reading this story that you didn't know before?

—What, if anything, will you do differently after reading this story?

—What surprised you in this story?

—Do you have a different view of this issue, or see a different way of dealing with it, after reading this story? Why or why not?

Credits

The stories in this book originally appeared in the following Youth Communication publications:

"Wish You Were Here," by Antwaun Garcia, *Represent*, September/October 2002; "Dealing With It," by Linda Rodriguez, *Represent*, September/October 2002; "Forgiving Doesn't Have to Mean Forgetting," by Rita Naranjo, *Represent*, November/December 2001; "My Hero Behind Bars," by Mary Fory, *New Youth Connections*, May/June 1999; "Staying Connected," by Youth Communication, *Represent*, September/October 2002; "Doomed to Repeat the Past?" by Antwaun Garcia, *Represent*, September/October 2002; "Seeing Through the Fog," by Anonymous, *New Youth Connections*, November 2008; "Tears of a Clown," by Eugene Han, *New Youth Connections*, December 2000; "Pen Pals," by Stevisha Taylor, *Represent*, September/October 2002; "45 Minutes on the Inside," by Mary Fory, *Represent*, September/October 2002; "Visiting Hours," by Linda Rodriguez, *Represent*, September/October 2002; "Out of Prison and Into My Life," by Dorena Belovet Ruff, *New Youth Connections*, November, 2006; "What Makes a Father?" by Youth Communication, *Represent*, May/June 2009; "Back in Touch After 14 Years," by Eric Benson, *Represent*, May/June 2009; "Getting Arrested Saved My Life," by Sandra Jimenez, *Represent*, March/April 2000; "Dreams for My Daughter," by Roger Griffin, Risemagazine.org, June 2007; "Bonding from Behind Bars," by Joanne Carroll, *Rise*, Summer 2008; "Signing Away My Son," by Deborah McCabe, *Rise*, Summer 2008; "Sentenced to Be Alone," by Natasha Santos, [Not published?]; "Special Delivery," by Derrick Alexander, *Rise*, Summer 2008; "I Lost My Rights But Not My Girls," by Bliss Edwards, *Rise*, Summer 2008; "Paying the Price," by Ayinde Fair, Risemagazine.org, August 2008; "Sugar Daddy," by Jermaine Archer, Risemagazine.org, April 2009; "'I'm Sorry': A Sex Offender Tells His Story," by Anonymous, *Represent*, July/August 2000.

About Youth Communication

Youth Communication, founded in 1980, is a nonprofit youth development program located in New York City whose mission is to teach writing, journalism, and leadership skills. The teenagers we train become writers for our websites and books and for two print magazines: *New Youth Connections,* a general-interest youth magazine, and *Represent,* a magazine by and for young people in foster care.

Each year, up to 100 young people participate in Youth Communication's school-year and summer journalism workshops, where they work under the direction of full-time professional editors. Most are African-American, Latino, or Asian, and many are recent immigrants. The opportunity to reach their peers with accurate portrayals of their lives and important self-help information motivates the young writers to create powerful stories.

Our goal is to run a strong youth development program in which teens produce high quality stories that inform and inspire their peers. Doing so requires us to be sensitive to the complicated lives and emotions of the teen participants while also providing an intellectually rigorous experience. We achieve that goal in the writing/teaching/editing relationship, which is the core of our program.

Our teaching and editorial process begins with discussions

between adult editors and the teen staff. In those meetings, the teens and the editors work together to identify the most important issues in the teens' lives and to figure out how those issues can be turned into stories that will resonate with teen readers.

Once story topics are chosen, students begin the process of crafting their stories. For a personal story, that means revisiting events in one's past to understand their significance for the future. For a commentary, it means developing a logical and persuasive point of view. For a reported story, it means gathering information through research and interviews. Students look inward and outward as they try to make sense of their experiences and the world around them and find the points of intersection between personal and social concerns. That process can take a few weeks or a few months. Stories frequently go through 10 or more drafts as students work under the guidance of their editors, the way any professional writer does.

Many of the students who walk through our doors have uneven skills, as a result of poor education, living under extremely stressful conditions, or coming from homes where English is a second language. Yet, to complete their stories, students must successfully perform a wide range of activities, including writing and rewriting, reading, discussion, reflection, research, interviewing, and typing. They must work as members of a team and they must accept individual responsibility. They learn to provide constructive criticism, and to accept it. They engage in explorations of truthfulness, fairness, and accuracy. They meet deadlines. They must develop the audacity to believe that they have something important to say and the humility to recognize that saying it well is not a process of instant gratification. Rather, it usually requires a long, hard struggle through many discussions and much rewriting.

It would be impossible to teach these skills and dispositions as separate, disconnected topics, like grammar, ethics, or assertiveness. However, we find that students make rapid progress when they are learning skills in the context of an inquiry that is personally significant to them and that will benefit their peers.

When teens publish their stories—in *New Youth Connections* and *Represent*, on the Web, and in other publications—they reach tens of thousands of teen and adult readers. Teachers, counselors, social workers, and other adults circulate the stories to young people in their classes and out-of-school youth programs. Adults tell us that teens in their programs—including many who are ordinarily resistant to reading—clamor for the stories. Teen readers report that the stories give them information they can't get anywhere else, and inspire them to reflect on their lives and open lines of communication with adults.

Writers usually participate in our program for one semester, though some stay much longer. Years later, many of them report that working here was a turning point in their lives—that it helped them acquire the confidence and skills that they needed for success in college and careers. Scores of our graduates have overcome tremendous obstacles to become journalists, writers, and novelists. They include National Book Award finalist and MacArthur Fellowship winner Edwidge Danticat, novelist Ernesto Quiñonez, writer Veronica Chambers, and *New York Times* reporter Rachel Swarns. Hundreds more are working in law, business, and other careers. Many are teachers, principals, and youth workers, and several have started nonprofit youth programs themselves and work as mentors—helping another generation of young people develop their skills and find their voices.

Youth Communication is a nonprofit educational corporation. Contributions are gratefully accepted and are tax deductible to the fullest extent of the law.

To make a contribution, or for information about our publications and programs, including our catalog of over 100 books and curricula for hard-to-reach teens, see www.youthcomm.org.

About the Editors

Autumn Spanne is the editor of *Represent*, Youth Communication's national magazine by and for youth in foster care. Prior to working at Youth Communication, Autumn was a reporter for newspapers in Massachusetts and California and spent five years teaching English and journalism on the Navajo Nation. She has a BA in literature from the University of California, Santa Cruz, an MS in journalism from Columbia University, and an MA in education from Western New Mexico University.

Nora McCarthy is a former editor of Youth Communication's two teen magazines: *Represent* and *New Youth Connections*. In 2005, she founded Rise, a nonprofit that trains parents to write about their experiences with the child welfare system in order to support parents and guide child welfare practitioners and policymakers. A graduate of the Medill School of Journalism at Northwestern University, Nora has written about youth and child welfare issues for Newsday, City Limits, and *Child Welfare Watch*.

Keith Hefner co-founded Youth Communication in 1980 and has directed it ever since. He is the recipient of the Luther P. Jackson Education Award from the New York Association of Black Journalists and a MacArthur Fellowship. He was also a Revson Fellow at Columbia University.

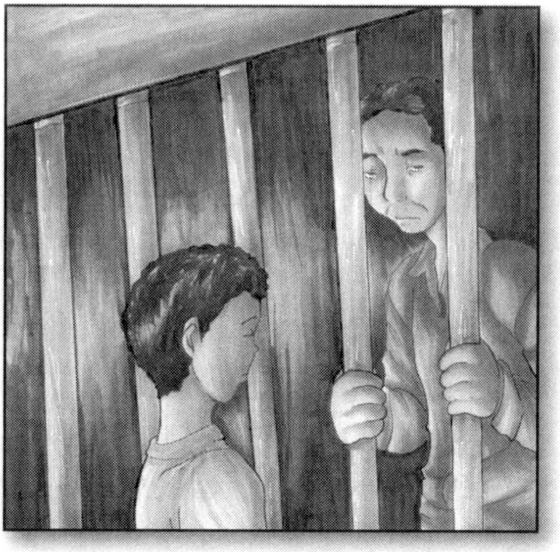

More Helpful Books From Youth Communication

Do You Have What It Takes? A Comprehensive Guide to Success After Foster Care. In this survival manual, current and former foster teens show how they prepared not only for the practical challenges they've faced on the road to independence, but also the emotional ones. Worksheets and exercises help foster teens plan for their future. Activity pages at the end of each chapter help social workers, independent living instructors, and other leaders use the stories with individuals or in groups. (Youth Communication)

The Struggle to Be Strong: True Stories by Teens About Overcoming Tough Times. Foreword by Veronica Chambers. Help young people identify and build on their own strengths with 30 personal stories about resiliency. (Free Spirit)

Depression, Anger, Sadness: Teens Write About Facing Difficult Emotions. Give teens the confidence they need to seek help when they need it. These teens write candidly about difficult emotional problems—such as depression, cutting, and domestic violence—and how they have tried to help themselves. (Youth Communication)

What Staff Need to Know: Teens Write About What Works. How can foster parents, group home staff, caseworkers, social workers, and teachers best help teens? These stories show how communication can be improved on both sides, and provide insight into what kinds of approaches and styles work best. (Youth Communication)

Out of the Shadows: Teens Write About Surviving Sexual Abuse. Help teens feel less alone and more hopeful about overcoming the trauma of sexual abuse. This collection includes first-person accounts by male and female survivors grappling with fear, shame, and guilt. (Youth Communication)

Just the Two of Us: Teens Write About Building Good Relationships. Show teens how to make and maintain healthy relationships (and avoid bad ones). Many teens in care have had poor role models and are emotionally vulnerable. These stories demonstrate good and bad choices teens make in friendship and romance. (Youth Communication)

The Fury Inside: Teens Write About Anger. Help teens manage their anger. These writers show how they got better control of their emotions and sought the support of others. (Youth Communication)

Always on the Move: Teens Write About Changing Homes and Staff. Help teens feel less alone with these stories about how their peers have coped with the painful experience of frequent placement changes, and turnover among staff and social workers. (Youth Communication)

Two Moms in My Heart: Teens Write About the Adoption Option. Teens will appreciate these stories by peers who describe how complicated the adoption experience can be—even when it should give them a more stable home than foster care. (Youth Communication)

My Secret Addiction: Teens Write About Cutting. These true accounts of cutting, or self-mutilation, offer a window into the personal and family situations that lead to this secret habit, and show how teens can get the help they need. (Youth Communication)

Growing Up Together: Teens Write About Being Parents. Give teens a realistic view of the conflicts and burdens of parenthood with these stories from real teen parents. The stories also reveal how teens grew as individuals by struggling to become responsible parents. (Youth Communication)

To order these and other books, go to:
www.youthcomm.org
or call 212-279-0708 x115

Y 362.829509 WISH

Wish you were here

NWEST

R4000545157

Discard

~~NORTHWEST~~
~~Atlanta-Fulton Public Library~~

CPSIA information
at www.ICGtesti
Printed in the US
FFOW02n13180
7781FF